The Poor Bartender

Richard Proteau

Copyright © 2016 Richard Proteau

All rights reserved.

ISBN:1537110837
ISBN-13:9781537110837

DEDICATION

To my wife Alison with love; because she stood by me unwavering while I sacrificed much in the name of truth and what is right.

CONTENTS

	Foreword	I
1	Introduction	1
2	Taxes: What give and what takes…	3
3	Who art thou?	8
4	Mortgages: Pay it and forget about it. Why?	15
5	Destroying the myths behind investment advice	24
6	The real cost/benefits of mutual funds	37
7	Other types of mutual funds	45
8	Leveraging: The doorway to losing your money	53
9	The truth about segregated funds	61
10	RRIF and income	69
11	Retirement and pension plans	91
12	Life Insurance	103
13	Group Insurance	123
14	Regulatory Environment	132
15	TFSA versus RRSP	142
16	Education	147
17	Beware of the prophets	150
18	The secret to not losing money	152

FOREWORD

When I wrote my first book "Unraveling the Universal Life Scam" https://www.amazon.com/Unraveling-Universal-Life-Shorter-Truth/dp/1503246167 https://store.kobobooks.com/en-CA/ebook/unraveling-the-universal-life-scam, I marveled at the misrepresentations plaguing the insurance industry. However I was never prepared to find evidence that these misrepresentations were organized and intentional. This constitutes fraud usually targeting the most vulnerable people in our society such as seniors… Having approached the government, requesting an intervention and investigation, I was even more surprised to see the government adopting a policy of "hear no evil; see no evil" As I continued my research and investigation, I came to the final conclusion that the regulating system adopted by the government through the influence of lobbyists, facilitated this kind of fraud. This is why I have named this type of fraud: "Regulated Fraud".

Regulated fraud is the greatest social and economic problem of our time. Someone was very right in stating that ""It is systemic and endemic," he went on, "and envelops the industry, the regulatory regimes and a great deal of the media" http://www.evidenceinvestor.co.uk/the-investing-industry-is-glad-that-most-of-us-are-clueless

Regulated fraud is a legal and governmental regime of wealth expropriation targeting the small and vulnerable investor. The only way out for the consumer is to opt out of this system.

When laws are a convenience for some and an obligation for others, there cannot be a just society; there cannot be a lawful society; conditions necessary for consumers to have confidence in the free market.

1 INTRODUCTION

Welcome to my establishment!

My name is John and I'll be your bartender tonight. Your name is Mike; you said. Nice to meet you!

Mike… you joked about not being able to afford a drink. Let me guess… Dealing with money problems, right? Money is tight…eh? Retirement is a dream which is getting further and further away from reality?

This is a common story, I'm telling you. We've all faced a bit of bad luck or hardship in our lives. Let me pay for this first drink if you are willing to listen to some of my stories about money. Usually I don't do this. Usually the customer does the paying and I do the listening but tonight I'll make an exception. I'll tell you everything I know about money. Even better; I'll also throw some wisdom for free.

Let's start with this drink. What I suggest Mike is something simple; one once; no two ounces of vodka, some ice, some club soda and a twist of lime. Nothing fancy you see, but I guarantee you it will do the job. It will even reduce the chances of a hangover if you abuse it. I'm telling you, as a bartender, I see a lesson here. Everybody is chasing the dream; the next thing, the next success, the next big win but nobody is preparing themselves for the hangover; the next loss.

We work so hard to make our way up the ladder that we are not thinking about falling or getting down.

That's how it is with money. There is a lot of help available about making money; about saving it. There is even a wealthy barber across the street who wrote a book about it. It's supposed to be good but how would I know? I have to tell you something …Mike. I know little about investing money or I wouldn't be wondering how much tips I can make out of my next customer. But when it comes down to losing money, this is an entirely different story.

I've seen it all and I've heard it all. All sorts of people have sat on these bar stools. From the farmer, fisherman to the six figures executives; they've all sat where you are now and every one of them had a story to tell. From the farmstead to the boardroom, it makes no differences. We can all make the wrong financial decisions.

I'm going to share with you their stories and maybe mine too. After tonight, I guarantee you; you will know more about how you can lose money when using the services and products offered by a financial industry that supposedly, is looking after you best interest. Understanding how not to lose money is the first step towards putting your financial affairs in order and surviving retirement. So drink, listen and don't worry. Like the drink I just served you, my tales won't be too complicated. In fact they'll be an exercise in simplicity.

2 TAXES: WHAT GIVES AND WHAT TAKES

The rich get to become richer by understanding taxation while the poor get to become poorer by not understanding it. (The Poor Bartender)

Where do I start? I know!

Look at that table over there... Used to be, every Saturday night at 8pm exactly, Henry would come and sit at this table. He would order a single Keith before going to work. He would sip his beer while catching the first hour of Hockey Night in Canada. Then he would have to go.

I remember he would say: "See you John. Have to go to work."

"Well at least, you won't have to watch the Leafs lose again," I would answer back to him.

"I swear one day the Leafs will make it to the finals and this will be the day I skip work to watch the game for the entire three periods. I'll even order a second beer."

"Yeah, keep the dream alive..."

No surprise here; this never happened. The Leafs winning... come on! Maybe this was best for him. Henry was struggling financially. He had two young children and his wife could not find a decent job that would cover daycare. It's not easy making a living in rural Nova Scotia. The only work he found was working the graveyard shift. He had to drive one hour and a half just to get to work. As you can see, Henry was a hard working man. He worked hard but the harder he worked, the more financial problems he had. Does this sound weird to you, Mike?

Financial planning is a bit like filling up a bucket. There are two ways of filling this bucket. First, you can pour water in it by getting a job and earning an income. The second way is for other people to pour water in your bucket. For example, if someone pays you rent or the bank pays you interest on an investment. The government also pours water in your bucket by paying you benefits. This is what happens when the provincial and federal governments pay children benefits to families.

At the bottom of the bucket there are two spouts. There is a spout that you control allowing you to take water out of the bucket for your needs and the needs of your family. There is also this other spout that you don't control. Through this spout, someone other than yourself has the right to take water out of your bucket without your permission. A good example is the government taking water out through what they call taxes.

We can state that the government gives and takes water at the same time. If I was to ask you if the level of water in the bucket is going to increase or decrease, you would probably point out to me that it will depend on whether or not the government is taking more water out than what it is putting in.

Pretty simple isn't it? But why poor people and families don't see this?

This was the problem with Henry. He would work overtime increasing his income from $40,000 to $42,000. This is a lot of hours away from those you love but it was a sacrifice he felt he needed to make in order to provide for his family.

"Great," he would say, "I now have $2,000 more than before.

Maybe I'll spoil the children. I am tired to tell them why they can't have what they want. For once, I want to see a smile of delight instead of disappointment written all over their faces."

He was however financially responsible and he knew how the government would want its share by taxing his $2,000 additional income. Out of this amount, the government would tax him and take $400. Not wanting to spend money that was not his own, he would put the $400 aside and he would spend the $1,600 left on his children; buying them the bicycle they wanted; getting some new clothes instead of used clothes; having a family night at the movies. When you have $1,600 and two children money won't last long.

But then, at a later date, he noticed something unusual. It became harder to make it to the end of the month. Every month, he would be short by about $100. How was this possible he would ask? Having no other choices, he would borrow the money to make it to the end of the month but then he would have to start paying interest; entering into what we call the down spiral of poverty.

"How can I be poorer when I worked harder and made $2,000 more; didn't spend it all in order to pay my taxes?" he would again wonder.

Do you know the answer Mike? I see that you don't. Remember that bucket we were talking about? The problem with Henry and his bucket is that he worried only about the water that the government was going to take out. He did not worry about the water that the government was putting in. If he did, he would have found that for every ounce of water he was personally adding to his bucket by earning more income, the government would reduce the amount it was putting in.

In other words, for every dollar of additional income, the government would tax it but it would also reduce the level of benefits paid to Henry. When he understood this, he checked again the amount of money he could really spend and he was shocked by what he found.

Because he had made $2,000 more in income this year, the federal government had reduced his federal child benefit by $500. His GST rebate went down by $100. He now had to pay $300 more in medications before being covered by pharmacare. He had lost his heating rebate of $200. His $2,000 of additional income had reduced his government benefits by $1,200. When he added the government income tax of $400 to this amount, the government share of his $2,000 income was really $1,600. This meant he had been wrong all along by thinking he could spend $1,600. He could only spend $400 since the rest belonged to the government. This is why he was short $100 per month.

Is this right? Is this wrong? I can't tell you. Would you work all this overtime to only put 20% of the additional income you are making in your pocket? I can't tell you that either. But this shows you that even the poor have to understand taxation or they will be spending money they don't have. We'll talk later about how Henry could have used this knowledge to save money.

Henry did not know what to do to get out of poverty. Earning more was not going to do it. They were however lucky. Henry and his wife lived on a hobby farm; in fact just up the road from my house. This hobby farm was the only reason why they were making it despite their financial situation. The hobby farm was providing them with a lot of the food they needed.

What happened to Henry and his wife? Even with the hobby farm they could not make it in Nova Scotia. When Henry started to look at the way he was taxed, he found something else and this disturbed him.

Despite being below the poverty line; which meant struggling to provide the basic necessities of life to his family; the Nova Scotia government was still taking almost $3,000 out of his bucket. When he compared this to other provinces, he found that, for the same family, Quebec did not take money out of the bucket but was instead pouring in an additional $2,500. Ontario was pouring in $1,800. So we are talking about a difference of $5,000 to $6,000 in benefits between Nova Scotia and other provinces. This is $500 less income per month. Living in Nova Scotia meant sacrificing his children health and chances! In fact, the Nova Scotia government through its taxation was really stealing Henry's benefits paid by the federal government such as the Canada Child Tax Benefit.

Henry decided he had enough of being poor and moved out of Nova Scotia. Last time I saw him, he told me he was now earning three times the money and was getting more benefits than when he was poor in Nova Scotia. See how regressive the taxation of families is in Nova Scotia and it is impacting all of us. Each time a family like Henry moves to another province, it means less money in our economy; less people in my bar. I know, I was not making much money out of Henry but it was a customer sitting at my table that is now empty.

So Mike, my first tip about not losing any money is:

"A fair tax system is a lie and you should always seek to understand how money gets into your bucket and how it is getting out of it. It is only then that you can maximize how much will be left in your bucket."

For more information on this subject:

(1) https://www.linkedin.com/pulse/good-industry-advocis-must-change-richard-proteau?trk=pulse_spock-articles
(2) https://fsconsumeralliance.wordpress.com/2016/02/03/nova-scotia-actively-creating-child-poverty/

3 WHO ART THOU?

"Other than the financial industry, I know of no other industry where there are so many people willing to help me with their free advice. Still I am left to wonder one thing. Why do I feel poorer every time I deal with these advisors?" (The Poor Bartender)

Welcome back Mike! Sit down; right here. I have a good drink and a good story for you.

The drink is named Dark 'n' Stormy. Perfect drink for the story I have for you. The story is named "The Feud".

But first, let's take care of this drink. What's in it? To make a Dark 'n' Stormy, you pour 2 ounces of dark rum, 3 ounces of ginger beer and ½ ounce of lime juice to freshen it up, if this is what you like, while adding some lime wedges as flotsam; a bit of wreckage representing our financial life. Perfect eh?

As I said, I have a good story for you. I call it "The Feud"; a feud which is still going on today. See this guy over there (I am pointing to the right corner of my establishment)? This is Robert and he sells insurance. See this other guy there (I am pointing to the left corner)? This is Paul and he sells mutual funds and he works for a bank.

There is a long term feud going between the two of them. At one point, the feud was so hot; they almost got into a fistfight right there in the middle of the floor. I had to divide the place in two. Robert is only allowed to sit on the right side and Paul has to sit on the left side.

What could push two reasonable men to this level of hostilities? When I found out why, it blew me away. See, Robert is life licensed and can only sell insurance products. This includes life insurance, annuities and Segregated Funds which are a bit like mutual funds except they have an insurance component which makes them more expensive. Robert cannot sell mutual funds.

Paul, since he works in a bank, is mutual fund licensed but cannot be life licensed and therefore cannot sell any life insurance products available to Robert.

The interesting thing is that they both offer the same service which is retirement advice. So this feud started quite simply. Competing for the same clients, Paul would tell a client not to trust Robert since he was selling more expensive products offering insurance they did not need. He would say to Robert's clients: "Why do you need a guarantee to protect your capital over 10 years when historically, if you stay in a mutual fund for 10 years, it is proven that at the end of this period, you'll get back more than your initial investment. You are wasting your money and you are paying insurance for nothing."

The clients would start to doubt Robert's advice. This would make Robert angry and he would retaliate by trying to prove his products were better. The situation quickly escalated; each one trying to outdo the other in discrediting the products they were selling. It did not take long before it got really personal when they started to discredit each other's reputation.

This is crazy when you think about it. Let's assume you want to build a house. Every contractor is licensed to build you a house but some contractors are only licensed to use the hammer while the other contractors are licensed to use the screwdriver. So whether you choose the first contractor or the second contractor, what kind of house do you think you're going to get? Chances are there will be a problem with your house because the proper tools could not be used.

Over time, you start having this feud between the two types of contractor with some saying that nails are better than screws while the others are stating the opposite. Crazy eh?

The same thing is happening with retirement planning. You are not offered the product that you need. You are offered the product that the advisor can sell to you. What happen if you need one particular product? Your need does not matter. The product that can be sold is instead recommended over the product that you need.

This is how these so called professionals are building your financial plan; with inadequate tools because they are not licensed to use all the tools required to provide you with the financial plan you need. Automatically, their advice becomes suspicious because it will be based on what they can sell instead of what you need.

By the way, this type of licensing is supposed to protect the consumers. What a joke! What you need to find is someone who has the two licenses; mutual funds and insurance. In other words, you need a contractor who is licensed to use the hammer and the screwdriver. But they are getting harder to find.

The reason is surprising. The mutual fund industry has been very aggressive in improving compliance. The insurance industry has been very resistant to any improvements on compliance. A lot of practices used in selling segregated funds are illegal when used to sell mutual funds. Selling mutual funds is getting more complicated because there are many more regulations.

As a result, those who hold both licenses are dropping their mutual funds license. Do you know why? It is to avoid compliance. Would you trust an advisor whose advice and products he is selling you is not based on what you need but on what takes less compliance?

As for Robert and Paul, they haven't talk to each others in years. It is not an easy thing to do in a small town like ours.

I 'm not done, Mike. Robert is calling himself a life insurance broker giving the impression that he is acting independently. In other words, he gives the impression that he is working for you. Last time, I had a big argument with Robert about this misrepresentation. It's like taking a cheap Scotch and passing it for an expensive Scotch by pouring it into an expensive bottle of Scotch.

Robert is not a broker. He is an insurance agent. I see it in your eyes. You are thinking: "Who cares!" But this is important. An insurer is responsible for the actions of its agents. It is not responsible for the actions of brokers. You can see the advantage that the insurers have in passing agents as brokers. Insurers can control and influence what an agent can sell while getting rid of any responsibilities associated with the sale of their products. There is a lot of influence exercised on an agent. As an agent, Robert is offered bonuses, trips, expensive gifts for selling a particular insurance product. If he was a broker acting for you this would be illegal because it would be considered a conflict of interest.

Why do I believe this is important? The answer is simple. An inefficient financial plan will cost you money. To make your financial plan more efficient, you have to rely on the advice of different professionals who are selling you the idea that the value of their advice is greater than the cost of their advice. If this was not the case, why would you use them? What is the chance their advice provides this value if right from the start they are misrepresenting who they are and what they can do?

Here is a story which illustrates this.

Cindy was a girl living five houses down from my house. She was the daughter of my good friend Tom. I know Tom very well. Each Sunday, I usually end up at his place to work on an old 1967 Pontiac Grand Prix we are trying to fix up. Anyway when Cindy finally graduated she did not know what to do. She did not want to work for someone. She had too much of an independent spirit.

She decided to attend a presentation made by a firm called Investors Group which was recruiting people to become financial advisors. Their sales pitch was really good. They were pushing the idea of a career where you had the flexibility and independence of running your own business. She decided this was the type of career she wanted and she became an Investors Group advisor.

It was not long before she was approaching family and friends asking them to invest with her. This is how they start you up, you know. Make a list of friends and family to approach. I did not mind. I like Cindy. I couldn't care less about Investors Group. I decided to support her and to open up an RRSP with her at Investors Group. For a year, I deposited $500 a month in a fund managed by this company. The return was not stellar but it was not bad either.

But then something strange happened. Usually Cindy would call me every three months to review my investments. She stopped calling me. When I called Investors Group, they told me that Cindy had left the industry and that I now had a new advisor.

"Impossible" I said. "Cindy would not quit without telling me. It's not like her. Her father raised her better than that." The new advisor started to argue with me on this. I hung up and I called Cindy's father who gave me Cindy's new phone number. Tom did not want to tell me if it was true that Cindy had quitted her career. He felt that it was better if she explained herself what had happened.

"Cindy, this is John" I said over the phone when I called her.

"Hi John."

"Is this true? Did you quit and you are not a financial advisor anymore?" I asked point blank.

"No it's not true."

"This is not what Investors Group is saying."

"Maybe their answer was not precise," she answered. I could feel a cool anger behind her voice. "I'm certain they meant to say that I left Investors Group but I'm still a financial advisor except that I'm with a new firm."

"Why did you leave them?"

"When I joined Investors Group, it was to become an independent business owner. The important word for me was independence which I felt was extremely important by allowing me to do what was best for my clients."

"You could not do this at Investors Group?"

"Not entirely. I discovered this when I reviewed the life policy of a client. He smoked cigars and he was considered a smoker by all insurers except one. The one insurer considered him a non smoker which was going to reduce his premium by more than $7,000. I wanted to submit an application with that insurer but I could not since this insurer was not part of the three insurers approved by Investors Group. I found out we were not allowed to deal outside of these three insurers."

"This is not right," I commented.

"Yes and no. I just wished I had known that prior signing with them and also knowing a lot of other stuff…"

"Such as?

"Well I found out, when I started to look at ending my relationship with Investors Group, that this was not my business after all that I was building. It was Investors Group's business. I should have read the fine print, I suppose. While I built this business using my time, my relationships and spending my money, contractually it was their business. Investor Group believes that my clients did not choose to do business with me but instead what they wanted was to do business with Investors Group."

"That's a pile of crap! The only reason I went with Investors Group is because of you. In fact, can I transfer my money back with you at your new firm?"

"Yes, but I would prefer that you did not."

"Why?"

"You are basically the property of Investors Group and I signed a non-compete agreement of two years. While I could transfer your funds because you called me and you suggested it, this is too dangerous. Investors Group could still sue me by implying the opposite and I don't have the money to defend myself legally. In two years I'll be happy to look after you…"

When I hung up I was mad. I am not the property of anyone. This is my money and it belongs to me and I am the only one who will decide who looks after it. We will talk about mutual funds fees later but I could have bought the same type of investments with much lower fees. The only reason I was paying the higher fees at Investor Group was to support Cindy.

It did not take me long before I decided to transfer my money out in an investment with no financial advisors and fund managers to skim my profits on what I was investing.

This leads to my second rule about losing money:

Tip 2: "There is only one person qualified to look after your money and it is yourself. There is only one person better qualified than yourself in looking after your money and it is a more knowledgeable version of yourself. If you delegate the responsibility of looking after your money to a third party, there is no value that can be derived from the advice of someone who is misrepresenting themselves right from the start."

4 MORTGAGES: PAY IT AND FORGET ABOUT IT. WHY?

A house is the most significant asset acquired by Canadians. The mortgage is the most significant liability taken on by Canadians. For some reason, house and mortgage are the least considered and managed part of financial planning. Could this be to the advantage of someone?" (The Poor Bartender)

Do you know what a Brass Monkey is? You may have heard the name in a song written by the Beastie Boys. They were singing about a 40-ounce bottle of malt liquor mixed with orange juice. The drink was introduced and named by Steve Doniger, an advertising executive, after an alleged World War II spy, named H. E. Rasske. The real drink is made of half oz rum, half oz vodka and four oz of orange juice. You toss the rum and vodka together and stir gently. You then pour the orange juice in. You shake well and finally you pour your ice in a highball or tall glass. That's a good drink with a lot of history behind it. The same could be said about mortgages.

I remember when I bought my home twenty years ago. I had scraped every penny I could to come up with the down payment. I worked two jobs; saved my bottles…anything that could be done I did it because this was the house I wanted.

When I had the down payment, I made an offer which was accepted. I then went to see my bank manager who was a friend I had known since primary school. I told him I needed a mortgage. He showed me some papers which needed to be signed and which I did not read. I did not ask one question because I trusted my bank manager. After all, in those days, a bank manager was seen as a person you could trust; particularly if he was your friend.

Fifteen years later, I am at the restaurant talking to a couple of my friends. They just got married and had bought a house. They were talking about their new home when I heard:

"Man, did we get a good deal on the mortgage. Almost 2% below the posted rate…"

"What do you mean 2% below the posted rate?" I asked a bit curious about what he was talking about.

"You know that the posted rate at the bank represents what the bank wants and not what they can offer?"

"No I did not. And I know, that all of these years, I've only been offered the posted rate. I always assumed, since my family has always been with this bank, that they were offering me their best rate. I am their best customer. I have everything with them…"

I was getting angry just thinking about this and when I got home I got the calculator out. My house had cost me about $100,000. Based on what I learned from my friend; a fact that I verified later; I could have gotten a mortgage rate 2% lower than what had been offered to me.

Calculator in hand, I realized I had paid $25,000 in interest I did not need to pay. If this $25,000 had been invested for my retirement it would easily be worth $50,000 today. This is a lot of money for me. This bank and my bank manager who were supposedly looking out for me; looking out for my retirement were in fact doing the opposite. They were taking advantage of my trust; they were taking money from my investments needed to provide for my retirement by charging me a higher interest rate on my mortgage. It was such an abuse of trust and such a conflict of interest.

This is when I understood that the only person you can trust with your money is yourself.

In a way, as consumers, we are all guilty of having created this problem. Listen to this. This is unbelievable!

"Johnny," I yelled across the bar to a man sitting alone at a table near the exit sign. "Come over here. Let's hear your story again."

Johnny left his seat reluctantly and for a moment he gave the impression that he was going make a run for it. But he made his way towards us.

"So listen to this. Johnny here received a renewal letter for his mortgage last month. His bank was so nice that they offered to renew his mortgage automatically at 5%. But Johnny had heard on the radio that a mortgage broker could get you a better rate than what banks were offering. So he called that broker. What did the broker offer you for a rate, Johnny?

"About 2.5%..."

"2.5%! This is half the rate offered by the bank. Were you angry Johnny?"

"Kind of..."

"Yes kind of...Do you think that our almost angry Johnny took the broker's offer by transferring his mortgage? Did you Johnny?

"No I didn't"

"That's right you did not. Instead you went back to the banker with this rate and what did the banker do?"

"He offered to match the rate…"

"He offered to match the rate and Johnny took it. He took the rate from the person that had been ripping him off for so many years instead of supporting the one person that had been honest with him which is the mortgage broker. The problem is simple. There are too many Johnnies out there and the banks know this. They don't need to change. They know that if they get caught stealing, these Johnnies will still put their mortgage with them."

Since there are no consequences why would the banks change? They will keep this up; trying to use these posted rates on their unsuspected clients.

When I realized I had been overcharged in accepting these posted rates, I started to review my whole mortgage. I came up with one interesting question. Why was I offered a five year rate? In fact, why were most Canadians offered a five year rate which we automatically accepted when the rates were at their highest? When I ran the numbers to compare how much interest I would have paid if I had accepted a variable rate versus a 5-year rate, I was astonished by the results.

I bought my home in 1990. The five year rate which I accepted was 14.3%. The variable rate was 14.8%. But the following year, the variable rate decreased to 9.8%. However I was locked in for 5 years at 14.3%. Interest rates continued to decrease and I continued to pay 14.3%. My bank manager did not contact me to tell me that maybe I should consider paying the mortgage penalties to get a better rate. Five years later, my mortgage was automatically renewed at 8.5%. The variable rate was 8.3% which continued to decrease while I was locked in at 8.5%. Over 15 years, by selecting a 5-year term, I paid $137,000 in interest. If I had selected a variable rate through the life of the mortgage, I would have paid $63,000 in interest. This is a $74,000 difference.

Add this to the $25,000 I lost because I had accepted a posted rate, I think I paid about $100,000 in interest that I did not have to pay. If this had been invested this would be worth today a minimum of $200,000. You understand why I'm not on track for my retirement.

Imagine how many people did the same mistake and we are all

asking ourselves why we don't have enough money for retirement!

Today, people still don't take the time to consider which term to select when taking on a mortgage. Interest rates are now different than what they were in 1990.

The 5-year best rate is 2.69% and the variable rate is 2.35%. Let me show you this on this napkin here. You don't mind if I scribble some numbers on your napkin?

Term	Variable	5year	10year
Spread (Posted - Posted VRM)	0	2.29	3.75
Posted Rates	2.35	4.64	6.1
Best Rates	2.35	2.69	3.84
Posted - Best	0	1.95	2.26
Spread (Best - Best VRM)	0	0.34	1.49
Multiple (posted spread/best spread)	0	6.74	2.52

Based on this information, which term would you choose?

Most brokers now recommend the variable rate because it is so low. I believe they are wrong. I believe that the interest spread is a key indicator of which rate offers the best value. The interest spread is the difference between the interest rate for the selected term versus the prime rate which we will assume to be equaled to the variable rate.

We see that the best 5-year rate is .34% higher than the variable rate. The 10-year rate is 1.49% higher. Now, let's look at the posted rates because this represents what the bank would like to offer. The spread for the 5-year term is 2.29% while the spread for the 10-year term is 3.75%. Basically, the 5-year spread for the best rate is 6.7 times lower than the spread for the 5-year posted rate. For the spread of the 10-year best rate, it is only 2.5 times lower. This means that banks are competing ferociously on the 5-year term best rate and are giving up a lot of profit in offering that rate.

Because of spreads, we now know that the 5-year rate is the better bargain. The best 5-year rate should be around 3.4% and instead it is 2.69%. I think the lenders are using the 5-year best rate as a loss leader to buy and attract business. It's no different than what I do on cheap night in order to get customers in the door.

Is the 5-year term better than the variable rate mortgage? To answer this we now have to look at rate trends. I lost money in 1990 because the interest trend was decreasing. I should have gone short with the selection of my term mortgage. A 1-year term would have been much better than the 5-year term.

I know what you are thinking. How can we predict what rates will do in the future? By the way, Mike, this is a good question.

You are absolutely right. It is impossible to predict rate trends in the future. However we can use common sense to assess the risk and opportunities associated with each trend. Let's look at three trends. First trend is decreasing mortgage rates. I think we can agree that rates are at their lowest. As a result, rates can't decrease much further and only in small increments. This tells us there is little opportunity.

If the variable rate decreases by .2% from 2.35% to 2.15%, the interest paid for the mortgage over 5 years would be $9,922 instead of $11,032. So you get a saving of about $1,100. To this saving, we need to add the savings you made by not investing in the 5-year term. That's about $1,500 more. So we can say that the amount of savings, if you believe interest rates will be decreasing, is about $2,500 per $100,000 slice of mortgage. I don't know about you but saving $2,500 seems pretty good to me. I'd rather this money be in my pocket than in the bank's vault.

One question remains. What is the risk you will be taking to make this saving? Before we look at this, let's look at the second trend; the neutral trend where interest rates are staying where they are.

In a neutral trend, the savings is the difference between the interests paid on the 5-year term versus the interest rate paid for the variable rate mortgage. As we stated before, the interest savings would be about $1,500. Now let's look at risk. Risk is interest rates increasing.

First, we know that the lenders have underpriced their 5-year term best rate. It means this rate could suddenly change by as much as .8% without any notice or change in the prime rate just because the lenders decided to change the way they are competing. On top of this, you have the risk of interest rates changing and increasing. The potential for increases is much greater. There is a lot of room to maneuver to increase rates! In the news, there are many warnings that this day is fast approaching…

We also have to account for procrastination. Imagine that the variable rate increases by .2%. What do you do? Is this temporary? Is the rate going to go back down? So you'll "nay, it's just temporary. It such a small increase I think I will wait." So you will probably decide not to convert to a 5-year term. You will wait in order to see what will happen. By the time you have reached this decision, rates have increased by another .2%.

Now you are sitting on the fence. Pressure is mounting. May be if you wait it out, the rate will go back down. Suddenly there is a third rate increase before you make your mind up of getting out of this variable rate mortgage by converting it to a 5-year term. When you look at the risk and what is probable, I would say that a rate increase of 1% is possible before you react. If this happens, it will cost about $5,000 more in interest per hundred thousand of mortgages.

I see it in your eyes. Knowing what I can lose against what I can gain still does not tell me which term to choose. You are right! The last piece is based on you and on probability. What is the probability that rates will decrease, stay the same or increase? If you were to ask what I believe, I would guess 25% they decrease, 25% they stay the same and 50% they increase. Using these probabilities to correct the gain and loss, we can define the loss at $2,500 if rates increase and the gain at $600 if rates decrease. Which one would you choose? I vote for the 5-year term.

Why? You still don't share my conclusion. Mortgage penalties??? Yes...right... I did not mention it... Well, you're asking for it. I'll throw more numbers at you. Mortgage penalties are indeed important. Most people don't buy a home to sell it in a few years but shit can happen.

Mortgage penalties are really important when interest rates are high and declining. Remember my mortgage in 1990 where I had a 14%+ mortgage rate for 5 years? Rates declined to 8% after this. Imagine if I had been forced to sell my home. Breaking my mortgage would have been extremely costly.

Now we are at the bottom of the mortgage rate curve and there is not a lot of room for rates to go lower. Here is an example. You take a 5-year term at 2.39% today and you sell your house in 4 years and the 1-year rate is 2.19%. On $100,000 mortgage, you are talking about an interest differential of $200. It would not apply and the lender would instead apply the 3 months penalty. That penalty would still be low.

The way I see it, I don't think there is a big risk with mortgage penalties versus risk of rates increasing at this moment.

Mike, I have to offer you a warning about mortgage penalties when dealing with the banks. You may force a bank to offer you a best rate instead of their posted rate but they are devious. The mortgage penalty will still be based on the posted rates where they are greater spreads between mortgage terms. Despite having a 5-year mortgage rate at 2.39%, they would use the posted rate of 4.6%. With the posted 1-year term at 3.5%, the interest rate differential is now $1,100... They are so sneaky... Why not use a mortgage broker who can set you up with a lender which does not use these deceptive practices?

Again trust no one; not even me. Check everything! Ask questions. The greatest mistake we make is to deal in absolutes. In financial planning, there is no such thing as a right or wrong financial decision; the goal should always be to reach the best financial decision built upon compromises. Financial planning is like buying a home. You have in your mind the perfect house and then reality sets in after you have viewed a few houses. This is when compromises have to be made. There is no right or wrong in selecting the best term mortgage for you. The question is what can you live with and live without?

My third tip is pretty simple: "Have a plan in mind to manage your mortgage. Even if you do not know the answers; just being aware of the questions can potentially save you hundreds of thousands of dollars. Anybody can make and save money; only the inquiring mind will not lose that money."

5 DESTROYING THE MYTHS BEHIND INVESTMENT ADVICE

> *Instead of basing financial advice on facts and observations, financial advisors base their investment recommendations on beliefs and rules of thumbs. Financial planning has more things in common with religion that it has with science. (The Poor Bartender)*

Mike! You are back! This makes me happy because I thought I scared you away with all these numbers during our mortgage discussion. I have some good info for you and I promise you this time; no numbers. Well… almost no numbers anyway. But first, let's deal with the important stuff. A man's thirst for knowledge is a curse unless it is quenched with a drink in hand. I'll make you a Hangman's Blood. This drink was created by Richard Hughes who used this drink in his 1929 novel, A High Wind in Jamaica. He described this drink "as being innocent as it looks, refreshing as it tastes, while having the property of increasing rather than allaying thirst." I think this sound exactly like money. The more money we have and the greater our thirst for money is.

You know the novelist Anthony Burgess? I'm using his recipe. You take a pint glass like this one. You pour and mix 1 ¼ oz of gin, whisky, rum, port and brandy. You then add stout beer to the desired level which is usually 5 oz and finally you top up with champagne. As Burgess said, it tastes very smooth, induces a somewhat metaphysical elation, and rarely leaves a hangover.

Now we are ready to talk about investing money and how people lose the money they invest by believing the myths that are presented to them.

The first myth sounds so good. Invest like Buffet! Doesn't that sound good? Who would not want to invest like the world's greatest investor? Who would not want to ride on his coattail? But this is lie. Buffet is not an investor like us. Investing money like us is putting $500 a month in an investment to build a retirement fund. Buffet is not such an investor; he is an opportunist. He buys companies and most of the time; he holds enough shares in the company to have a seat on its board. Does that sound like you and me? So why are people telling us to invest like him? It's certainly catchy. We are sold this dream where you can become as successful as Buffet. It's easier to sell this dream than telling us how we will have to scratch and save every penny we can and still we will not be able to have the retirement of our dreams.

By selling us the dream, they avoid telling us the compromises which we will have to make. But this is the best way to lose money. A compromise made today is a lot less painful than a compromise made tomorrow. A compromise ignored results in many dollars lost.

This is why you never invest like Buffet. Buffet can take a lot of risks. Do you think that if he loses 20% of his money, he will worry about how he is going to pay the mortgage or that he won't be able to retire? If you and I lose 20% of our money, our retirement will be pushed back by another 10 years.

The greatest difference between us and Buffet is that we save money in order to buy investments that will provide us the desired income at a future date. Investing for income which you and I are doing versus investing for growth is entirely different. Our investment choices are defined by risk. His investment choices are defined by opportunities. The day you invest like Buffet is the day you don't have to worry about retirement anymore… or money for that matter…

Buffet buys stocks and he thinks of these stocks as businesses. We don't buy stocks. We buy mutual funds and we have no influence on the stocks these mutual funds buy. You cannot reduce portfolio turnover. You can't tell the fund manager to buy or sell a particular stock. This is out of your hands. The fund manager makes the decision. We can't ignore market forecasts. We can't weather a loss because we are on the clock. We will see later what this means from a financial planning perspective.

So my fourth tip is: "Do not invest like Buffet because your investment decisions are dictated by compromises while Buffet's decisions are dictated by opportunities."

So Mike, how is your drink? Want another one? Yes, you do? Good, it will help with the second myth.... The second myth is "Buy and Hold". Buy and Hold is a passive investment strategy where you buy stocks to hold them for a long period of time, regardless of whether the market goes down or goes up. Right from the start we have a problem. "Buy and Hold" applies to stocks but somehow this concept made its way into investing in mutual funds which is entirely different.

Everyone understands that over a long term horizon, equities provide a higher return than other asset classes such as bonds. The debate is about whether a buy and hold strategy is actually superior to an active investment strategy.

The advisors and the fund managers all believe and promote the idea of buying and holding to a mutual fund for 10 or 15 years no matter what. Buffett is again used as an example by the financial industry of why you should buy and hold on to that mutual fund. It does not matter if there is good news or bad news; you hold on to your mutual fund even if there is a god dam meteor about to strike the earth. Crazy eh!

Mike you have to wonder why the fund managers want us to buy and hold and believe me it's not for our best interest. The reasons when you think about it are quite obvious…

There is more commission for the advisor and the fund manager;

if you have your money in cash they don't get much of a commission. The more you are invested the more sales and service commission they get.

It's less expensive for the fund and the advisor. Rebalancing cost time to the advisor which he does not have since he wants to use that time to sell more instead of servicing you. Rebalancing and redemptions have a tremendous impact on the performance of the fund increasing transaction costs.

By convincing us to buy and hold, the fund manager can reduce the impact of cash drag on the overall performance of the fund. The less cash they need to keep in hand to deal with redemptions, the less impact it will have on the performance of the fund.

It reduces tax cost. When the fund sells shares, if it is not a RRSP, there is a taxable disposition and tax payable which reduces the return of the fund. Finally they lose control of your money.

Mike, let me ask you this question. Based on this information should we be skeptical about how good this "Buy and Hold" strategy is?

To justify the "Buy and Hold" strategy, the financial industry has literally created a boogey man. This boogey man has a name and it is called "Market Timing". As soon as you want to sell some of the equity you have in order to protect the gain you've made, they will say you are trying to use Market Timing. With pseudo numbers, they will say that it is impossible to consistently achieve above average returns, on a risk-adjusted basis, according to the efficient market hypothesis. Sounds important, right? They must know what they are talking about!

They will continue by telling you that all investors have access to information that will fairly value a security at all times. Therefore, it is pointless to make decisions that might result in any active management. The "Buy and Hold technique" is a long-term investment strategy. If the market goes down in the near future, then it should be an acceptable outcome to you. You have to believe that the longer trend will be positive. Selling or buying mutual funds because you think the market is going to move up or down is not a valid reason for selling or buying. Selling after the market has plummeted or buying after the market has skyrocketed is what is going to happen if we actively manage our money. This is what we, the poor uneducated clients, are doomed to do.

Since the market timing strategy implies the ability to get into and out of sectors, assets or markets at the right time, they will tell us it is impossible for us to buy low and sell high. The reverse will happen. We are so stupid. They will try to convince us that we are doomed to buy high and sell low because our behavior is usually driven by emotions instead of logic.

Mike, it is such a compelling argument. We have to be protected against ourselves. The fund managers and financial advisors are the heroes who will save us…in return for a hefty commission…

Think about it, Mike. These advisors and fund managers are asking you to be happy with losing 50% of your investment as it happened in 2008 and do nothing about it. Isn't that nut? But people are buying that crap...

Let me tell you a story. I was invited by an advisor to attend an investment seminar where some of the fund managers of Manulife were going to be present. They were going to tell us everything about investing. This was in 2010. We had been through a bad period where the TSX Index went from a high of 15,073 plunging to a value of 7,567 by March 9, 2009. I remember that date exactly… So I expected something new from this seminar. I expected these fund managers to say: "we've learned something from this." They did not. They made the same speech. They started to say that the way to build up savings was to "Buy and Hold". It pissed me off. You know, I lost more than 50% of my money to a market correction. I wanted to know how to keep my wealth and not losing it before I reach retirement.

So I put my hand up to ask a simple question. The young fund manager with cheeks as bare as his ass looked up and said:

"You have a question?"

"Damn sure I have a question. What demographics…" See I do know some big words…. "What demographics is your fund targeting?"

"What do you mean?"

"I would guess that all of us sitting around this table are about 55 of age. This means we all have retirement on our mind; we all want to retire in about 10 years… we hope anyway…So how are we supposed to "Buy and Hold?""

"I don't know what you are saying. This is in 10 years… and history has shown that…"

"I don't give a damn about history. The history I am talking about is the history where I lose 50% of my money. What I am saying is that we are all going to have to sell to retire and this is approaching fast. Are you suggesting we forget about this; forget everything about what can happen in and between; bet the whole farm on a specific point in time; hoping that in that one particular moment, the stars align correctly for us to retire. It can't be. You would not be stupid enough to say this. Does it mean, if we are doing the buying and the holding, that you are going to do the selling for us? Are you going to preserve any growth to ensure that in 10 years we have the liquidities to take an income? If this is the case, I don't see how you can invest us and pool our funds with a bunch of thirty years old that can hold these funds for 30 years. So you must have a fund for people like us who are approaching retirement where we will be doing the holding and where you will be paid to do the selling…"

"We don't have this and we don't do this…"

"So you are telling us that if a fund goes up by 50% and we are 10 years from retirement we should do nothing and you will do nothing?"

Anyway this presentation did not go well. Think about it Mike. Let's assume you retirement plan is based on a 5% investment return. To retire in 10 years, you have to earn 5% on your money. The day after you have done this plan, it's a great day for the market and the fund goes up by 25%. This is 5 years worth of planned return. You are 5 years ahead of plan and the fund manager is telling you to hold. If you take all of your cash out and invest in something that is less risky and you earn 3% for the 5 years, it would take 8 years before you are behind what you have planned. If you are 30 years old and the market goes up 25%, you may decide to ignore this and hold even if it is wrong but at least you got time. We don't! Demographics show that the majority of people who have money invested are not thirty year old. They are my age and we can't hold.

There is nothing wrong with Market Timing because it is unavoidable anyway. Our retirement plan when you think about it is built towards the single greatest Marking Timing event which is when you have to start to withdraw your money to retire. I would say it's better to take many little steps towards this by protecting your gains then betting the whole farm entirely on one point in time.

So my fifth tip is: First get yourself a retirement/investment plan. Never measure what the market does only measure where you are in relation to your plan as this is the only thing that matters. Make your decision not on what the market does but where you are in relation to your plan. Never be afraid to withdraw from the market when you are ahead of your plan.

We are almost done Mike. Here is another myth for you. The way we are sold investments is on the basis that the stock market is able to take in any amount of money. We are given the impression that the market can expand forever. We are influenced in believing that one dollar of money invested in the market will create at a minimum, one dollar of value on the long term.

Look at my bar. If the first guy that comes in wants to invest one dollar in my bar, there are no problems. That one dollar, I can use it to create value by buying or fixing equipment to become more efficient; to cut my cost down... This creates value. But if the next thousands of customers also want to invest in my bar, the changes or what I can do with that money will have less and less impact on efficiency or cost. Their investment will create less and less value. But I can still charge the same price because of the demand.

When this point is passed, any change in the value of my bar is purely based on the demand to invest in it. It has nothing to do anymore with the value or profit that the bar can make. This value is not real anymore. It's purely speculative.

The same thing applies to the market. When the market increases in value, this first change is a reflection of increased or decreased value. But passed a certain point, it is just pure speculation and this becomes very dangerous when you link this to demographics.

I've read a lot about demographics because I now understand how the current demographics represent one of the most important single events in human history. It's changing everything and it is global in nature. Every country has the same problems. Too many old people for the number of young people and we won't simply die.

What does it mean to the world of investing? Think about it. We all don't have enough money to retire. You would think this means that as a whole we don't have much money to invest. This is wrong; quite the contrary. While we don't have much money individually there are so many of us. Collectively we have a lot of money and we are all looking for the same type of investment; something that provides a good return with little risks as possible. What are the choices? Not too many, I can tell you. Interest rates are too low so guaranteed investment certificates are out of question. Bonds have little to offer. We only have equity left as a choice.

We are faced with the basic law of supply and demand. I've researched this and here is what I can tell you. Supply and demand is perhaps one of the most fundamental concepts of economics and it is the backbone of a market economy. Demand refers to how much of a product or service is desired by buyers. In our case, the quantity demanded is the amount of investments people are willing to buy at a certain price; the relationship between price and quantity demanded is known as the demand relationship.

Supply on the other hand represents how much the market can offer. The quantity supplied refers to the amount of investments producers are willing to supply when receiving a certain price. The correlation between price and how much of a good or service is supplied to the market is known as the supply relationship. The price of an Investment Index such as the Toronto Stock Exchange (TSX) is therefore a reflection of supply and demand.

Let us take a closer look at the law of demand and the law of supply.

The law of demand states that, if all other factors are equal, the higher the price of a good, the less people will demand that good. It means that the higher the price, the lower the quantity demanded. The amount of a product that buyers purchase at a higher price is less because as the price of a good goes up, so does the opportunity cost of buying that good. They can't purchase this product without making a sacrifice and buying less of another product.

When supply and demand are equal the economy is said to be at equilibrium. At this point, the allocation of a product is at its most efficient because the amount of products being supplied is exactly the same as the amount of products being demanded. In the investment world, at a given price, suppliers of investments are selling all the investments that they have produced and investors are getting all the investments that they are demanding.

Demand and supply cannot be ignored except this is exactly what we do when it comes down to investing. Somehow this law is ignored and this will always result in huge consequences. It is the origin of the subprime mortgage crisis which almost destroyed the global economy. At the beginning, good mortgages were packaged as investments and because of demographics everybody wanted them. They provided good returns and little risks.

Investors were screaming for more. However the supply was limited because there are only so many people who had the financial capacity to buy a house or refinance a mortgage. To meet the demand, the rules were relaxed. It became easier to get a mortgage. With more homebuyers, home prices went up. Current homeowners were then able to refinance. Now the suppliers of investments could package all these risky mortgages into investments while getting the same or even a better price. Demand kept increasing and more bad mortgages were packaged as good investments. This demand continued until everything crashed and this excess demand was erased. In the end, the market did what it was supposed to do and it reached equilibrium by erasing the wealth of the regular investor.

Let's get back to investing into the equity market…The demand for an investment is therefore highly fueled by demographics. The demand for investments is extremely high. Because of interest rates, the variety of investments available is very limited. We are all pouring our money in the same investment. The price of the supply increases and still there is too much money. We are still buying more fuelling speculation. The market has to be efficient and supply and demand have to move towards equilibrium. How is this going to happen?

Normally when the market heats up with the prices getting higher, we should invest less reducing the demand. This is not happening because of the dollar cost averaging concept promoted by the financial industry. When is the last time your advisor called you to tell you he is changing you deposit allocations? Why would anyone buy the TSX at 15,000+ like it happened in 2008? Think about it Mike. I know people, because of dollar cost averaging, who have continued to invest in Canadian equity when the market was at 15,000. Everybody knew the market was overpriced. However the advisor told them to stick to the course. Now 10 years later, the market is still not above 15,000. Maybe in 10 years, the market will reach that level again. This means these deposits are worthless and contribute nothing to your future retirement. In fact they drag down your investment return and the money you will have available at retirement. What a waste of money! But the advisor got his commission and this is what is important!

When is the last time you bought something that was clearly overpriced? This is what we do all the time as investors. We continue to buy the same mutual fund automatically with our monthly deposit no matter what; no matter the cost. Demand remains the same when it should be decreasing. Again the financial industry has convinced us to act against our best interest.

When the market can't reach equilibrium, the market can only crash.

Supply should also increase through redemptions. Again this is not happening. People are holding to their mutual fund because they are following their financial advisor's advice which is to "Buy and Hold". As a result, the market cannot reach equilibrium on this side either. The only way for the market to reach equilibrium is to crash and erase some of that money. By crashing the market is doing exactly what it is supposed to do by erasing some of the wealth in order to ease the demand. The question is who is going to lose that wealth? The answer is simple and it is the people or the sheep that are holding to their investments when they should be selling. In fact they create a pool of stable money that the speculators can use to hedge their bets.

My sixth tip for you is important to understand if you don't want to lose money. There is nothing wrong in selling an investment to protect a gain. This has nothing to do with Market Timing. It's all about following a plan. Because of demographics if you do like everyone else instead of acting for yourself, it is guaranteed that you will lose money. Investing is a competition that only the few who actively manage their gains by limiting their losses can win.

Another myth I have for you is that churning on mutual funds does not impact your mutual fund investment. What a great lie! Churning happens when a stockbroker makes trades on your account to generate large commission. Basically for each trade made the stockbroker makes a commission and this is deducted from your investment. It does not take long for these commissions to decimate and destroy your investment.

A well known case is about this widow who was with the Royal

Bank. Her broker bought 500 shares of Royal Bank stock at $30.25 and then sold the same stock at $30.75 and $30.88. After deducting the broker's $528 commission, she was left with a loss of $246. Imagine if this is repeated over and over; how fast your investment will disappear. The widow sued and an out of court settlement was reached but she was lucky. How many of us can spend thousands of dollars in legal fees when our money was stolen through churning? This is how they get away with it.

With mutual funds, the industry is saying that churning is not a problem. If an advisor transfers your funds to another fund, the fees will likely be the same. The only thing that will change is the deferred charges applying to your money. There will be new deferred charges and it is only when you have to withdraw your money that you will have to pay these charges which can be quite high.

But here is the truth. Do you think that a fund transfer, whose only purpose is to generate commission, even if the fees don't change, will be good for you? Do you think that the advice you are receiving at this point is objective? Do you think this is done for your benefit?

As I mentioned before, the only thing that matters is your financial plan. The first thing you should accept with planning is that things will not happen as expected and as planned. For a financial plan to work you need to adapt and make the right changes. You can't do this if you are faced with deferred charges. As a result churning on mutual funds is as bad as churning with stocks. You will lose your money.

My final myth is that by buying a mutual fund, I am protected from fraud. Sorry Mike this is not true. It seems weird to say that mutual funds could become part of an investment scam since they are closely regulated because of their popularity. Recent scandals have proven that a mutual fund can become an investment scam. The scam usually involves fund company insiders who allow selected investors to have special privileges not available to other investors. For example, these special investors could be allowed to enter trades long after the trading deadline had passed when the fund's performance for the day is known. It's like making a bet when the winning number is known. These practices will result in a reduced return for the average fund investor. Unfortunately, it is very difficult, if not impossible for investors to know if their mutual fund company is engaged in this scam.

My seventh tip is the only tip from Warren Buffet that applies to us: "Rule No.1: Never lose money. Rule No.2: Never forget rule No.1."

6 THE REAL COST/BENEFITS OF MUTUAL FUNDS

> *Most Canadians believe that buying the most expensive investment providing the least value is somehow the path to a successful retirement. The numbers and results speak for themselves... (The Poor Bartender)*

Everybody knows what a Tom Collins is. It is such a well known drink. Not a lot of people know The Tom Collins Hoax of 1874. At that time, people in the United States would start the hoax by asking someone "Have you seen Tom Collins?" The person who was asked this question would answer that they did not know a Tom Collins. The speaker would then claim that Tom Collins was talking about them to other people. In fact Tom Collins was just around the corner. The speaker would then encourage his victim to act foolishly by reacting to his hoax believing that it was real. The goal was to get the victim of this hoax to become so angry at the idea of someone talking about them that they would rush off to find and confront this Tom Collins. Newspapers even got onto this hoax by printing stories containing false sightings of Tom Collins. This hoax became so famous that it was mentioned in several music hall songs.

The story of this hoax is a great introduction to mutual funds fees but first let me make you a Tom Collins. For this we use ice cubes, 2 oz. dry gin, 2 oz. lemon juice, 1 teaspoon sugar, soda water, a slice of lemon and 1 cherry. We first put the ice in a large glass. We add the mixture of gin, lemon juice and sugar. We top up with soda water and stir well. Let me put in a lemon slice, cherry and your drink is ready, voila!

Let me ask you a question. Why are we doing so poorly with our retirement savings? Is it because we are not saving enough; spending too much? If you listen to the politicians and the financial industry, it's always our fault. However I have already shown you how our trust in the financial industry is costing us a lot of money. I hope you remember what I told you about mortgages…

I can tell you that the cost of owning a mutual fund is far greater than what meets the eye. This cost is killing our retirement savings while the industry is making billions of profits on our backs. We're talking about $20 billion annually taken from hard working Canadians in the form of investment management fees (MER) and other expenses. The government is not doing anything because it is also getting its share through taxes which are buried and hidden from us. Buying a mutual fund is like buying gas. Try and figure how much money you are truly paying in taxes. Good luck with this…

This is primarily due to two reasons. First, only about half of the total cost is reported in the disclosed MER. In other words, when other hidden fees are considered, they can more than double the value of the disclosed MER. Another factor often missed is the power of compounding fees where small increases in MER can become material over time. Compounding returns is the engine of our retirement. Compounding expenses are the brakes removing any momentum out of our retirement.

For example, a MER of 2% percent may not seem like much but over time it will reduce your retirement nest egg by about $280,000 over 30 years assuming that you are saving $10,000 annually and you are earning a 7% rate of return. Think about it. Instead of retiring with $945,000, you are left with $665,000. Now I want you to be honest here. What would you expect from someone you are paying $280,000? I believe you would have the right to expect a stellar performance. Have fund managers and advisors deliver this amazing performance?

Well, you can go check the answer on SPIVA Canada which compares the performance of Canadian mutual funds against their indexes. They are basically the scorekeeper of this industry and I can tell you the score is not in favor of actively managed Mutual Funds and fund managers. However I skipped one important topic. What is an Index Fund? An Index Fund is a type of mutual fund with a portfolio constructed to match or track the components of a market index such as the Toronto Stock Exchange (TSX). Index funds are usually cheaper than regular mutual funds

But I see you are curious. What is the score? The score is that 90% of all actively managed Mutual Funds with the TSX as the reference have done worst than this index. So you paid $280,000 to fund managers and advisors who have continuously failed you. They have provided no value and you would have done better by buying an Index fund. I think it is time they get fired or at least they get a pay cut.

But we are not finished. The 2% I quoted you is not realistic. It's way too low. Canada has the most expensive Mutual Funds in the world with an average MER of 2.55%. Think about it. This means 50% of Mutual Funds are more expensive than 2.55%. Just an increase of .25% in the MER, over 2%, will cost you $30,000 over 30 years. For some reasons, there are people who accept to pay a MER of more than 3% for brand name Mutual Funds. They don't stand a chance.

Another thing that is weird in Canada is that in average, balanced funds are more expensive than equity funds. You are paying more to have a bond component and this does not make sense. As a result, you have to be extremely careful in selecting a balanced fund. It must have a MER below 2.5%. This is because by being conservative, you already are sacrificing some possible returns to reduce risk. You don't want to add more MER to this sacrifice.

If at least the MER was the only expense reducing your nest egg but I told you before it is only the tip of the iceberg. Your retirement nest egg is the Titanic and it is on a crash course towards destiny. You can either drink and be merry and ignore what I am about to tell you or you start looking for that iceberg knowing that what you see above the water is a fraction of what is under the water. So what are these expenses not included in the MER?

There is the cash drag. This is the amount of cash a fund holds in order to maintain liquidity which is needed to fund potential redemptions. Many studies have indicated that cash drag can reduce the fund performance by as much as 83 basis points per year. But let's be conservative and assign a value of .5% to cash drag.

There are the transaction costs which are associated with the buying and selling of stocks by fund managers. Transaction costs can be fees paid to brokers and access to their research and analysis. These broker fees are around .25%. Transactions cost also includes market impact cost. This is a tricky one. A mutual fund manager buys large amount of stocks and this will influence the price of the stock when the order is filled. Again when the demand is high in what direction does the price move? Market impact cost is a loss for mutual fund investors like us because we get uncompetitive pricing on both the buy and sell side of stock transactions. Another factor is the bid/ask spread, which is the difference in price between what the dealer will buy and sell a stock. That spread is very small but it still represents another .25 basis points per year. All of these fees add up. I found a 2007 study which evaluated that cost and found that it was about 1.44% per year. Again we will be conservative and we will assign a value of 1%.

Another type of unreported cost is capital gain taxes. Now we could ignore this as this impacts only mutual funds held outside a registered account. Most Canadians like you and me don't fully use all of the room we have for RRSP and TFSA so we simply don't rely on unregistered mutual funds for our retirement. Still if you ever get rich this is something you have to consider. Without understanding how mutual funds are taxed you will never be able to have an effective investment plan.

Mutual Funds distribute income to its unit holders to reduce the overall taxes paid by the fund.

Usually a mutual fund trust is taxed at a rate equivalent to the highest personal tax rate. Any income retained by a mutual fund would therefore be subject to more tax than if it were taxed in our hands. This is why this income is distributed to us. For example, if there is stocks turnover, the capital gains associated with the sale of the stocks will be passed on directly to us. There has been an estimate made that this tax could cost 1 percent per year for a typical equity fund. Removing turnover is difficult for a mutual fund. Remember that we invest in funds with the best performance. Fund managers know this and they realize they must have investments that increase in value which will accumulate unrealized gains. When these gains are realized by selling the investment, the owners of the fund will have to pay capital gains taxes. The catch is that these gains apply to the fund and if you bought the fund after it appreciated in value, you will still be on the hook for the capital gain taxes.

There is a good story that just came out. Bernie Bellan bought a mutual fund from Royal Bank. He owned that fund for 10 years and for that period of time there was little capital gain distributions. This meant the fund had been good at managing turnover. Then just this year he receives his T3 tax slip and he was shocked to see he was on the hook for about $22,000 in capital gains. What happened was the fund had replaced the stocks with RBC's own mutual funds. It was legitimate since the unit holders had agreed to this by voting for this change. However RBC had never informed the unit holders of this potential gain and tax. The excuse of RBC was that it was impossible to predict this capital gain because of volatility. Can you believe this? Where were the financial advisors who sold these funds? Imagine the people who unlike Bellan did not hold this fund for ten years and were on the hook for the same capital gain.

Mike if we summarize all of this, it is believed that these hidden expenses create an estimated total MER of 4.52 percent for a taxable account and a total MER of 3.52 percent for non-taxable accounts such as RRSPs.

The total cost of mutual fund ownership lowers the 7% annual rate of return to 3.48%. In our example, we saw that instead of retiring with $945,000, the existence of a MER of 2% would reduce your retirement nest egg to $665,000. Now by adding the hidden cost, your nest egg will have a value of $515,000 after 30 years. This is $430,000 gone in fees…

An easy way to see how MER can decimate an investment is to use "The Rule of 40". It is a way for mutual fund investors to estimate the number of years it takes for a Management Expense Ratio (MER) to consume a third of the initial investment. You start by dividing the number 40 by your fund's MER and that tells you how many years it will take for a third of the investment to be lost through fees. For a MER of 2% you divide 40 by 2 to get 20 years. When you add the hidden expenses, a fund with a total MER of 3.5% would take just 11.5 years to eat a third of your investment nest egg.

As a result, the MER of a mutual fund is the most dependable predictor of performance. Studies have shown that funds with the lowest MER produced the highest total returns. Funds with the most expensive MER produced returns which are the lowest.

Why is the government not intervening to limit the ability of mutual funds in charging these expensive fees? The reason may surprise you. The government is getting a piece of the action by charging GST and HST on mutual funds. The government is blaming us for not saving enough money for retirement and it is taxing us through a back door. In fact, taxes are an important factor in making mutual fund fees as high as they are. GST is applied on the operating and management expenses a fund has, and in provinces with an HST, this tax also applies.

Imagine Mike that an investor puts $5,000 annually for 25 years in a mutual fund with an average annual return of 6% per cent and a MER of 2 per cent. The HST and GST tax will cost this investor $7,300. At $10,000 a year, the cost will double up.

Mike, I hope you are now convinced. When you're comparing investments that are similar, one of the first things if not the only thing you should look at are the investment fees. How much will it cost to buy into this investment? What are the annual fees going to be? This can easily save you tens of thousands of dollars of savings for your retirement.

The good news is that you don't have to be an expert to get an investment with low fees. Your first choice should be to select an Index fund. This does not mean you buy and hold these Index mutual funds. We will talk later about how to actively manage your Index funds.

The evidence is obvious for everyone to see. The less you pay to invest, the greater your net returns will be. The financial industry knows this all too well. However since it benefits from these high fees, it does all it can and will do everything to maintain them. The financial industry's best weapon as we shall see is the financial advisor. This explains why the industry is so opposed against the disclosure of fees and disclosure of conflicts of interest by advisors. The industry is also against the principle of fiduciary duty that a financial advisor should owe you. The battle lines are drawn. On one side there is a financial industry who wants to sell you the product that will generate the most profits to them. On the other side, a few people are fighting back arguing that what is sold to consumers should be the best product suited for their needs at a reasonable price.

The belief of the financial industry is that you and I can only benefit from financial advice if we are charged outrageous fees and sold products that we don't need. Crazy eh!

Fees matter. Let me tell the story of the twins. The first twin Maria worked for a big company which was offering a defined contribution plan. We will talk about pension plans later. The second twin, Sue worked for a small business which was only offering a RRSP matching plan. Anyway they both were contributing the same amount towards their retirement which was about $2,500. They both invested in the same type of fund and it happened that the rate of return they both earned to age 65 was a gross rate of return of 6%. What was amazing is that the pension of Maria was $40,000 higher than the RRSP of Sue. To have the same level of retirement than Maria, Sue would have to work and contribute to her RRSP for another 3 years. The only difference between Maria and Sue retirement plan was the level of fees they paid. Sue paid a fee three times higher than Maria.

My eighth tip should not surprise you. "The greatest source of loss when you invest is management fees. As a result, this should be your primary and main concern. Do not let financial advisors divert your attention on things that don't matter such as mutual fund rankings…"

7 OTHER TYPES OF MUTUAL FUNDS

Mutual funds make investing easy; we are unburdened from looking after our own retirement while being burdened to look after the retirement of advisors and fund managers by paying ridiculously high fees that provide absolutely no value… (The Poor Bartender)

Don't worry Mike, we are almost done with mutual funds. It is a long topic but we have to go through it before I reveal to you the secret sauce to not losing money when you invest.

Do you know that the Bloody Ceasar is a Canadian cocktail? This is the drink I want to make for you today. The Bloody Caesar was invented in 1969 in Calgary, by bartender Walter Chell at the Westin Hotel. He had been asked to come up with a drink to commemorate the opening of Marco's, the hotel's Italian restaurant. Using the Italian cuisine for inspiration, he came up with a mixture of mashed clams, tomato juice, vodka, Worcestershire sauce, salt, and pepper. Garnishing it with a celery stick, he named this new drink for the Roman Emperor "Bloody Caesar". Later, the Mott Company went on to develop what we know now as "clamato" juice. This made this drink very popular and about 250 million Mott's Clamato Caesars are consumed annually.

To make a Bloody Caesar is simple: 1 oz Vodka, Clamato juice, 1 dash Worcestershire sauce, 1 dash Tabasco sauce, Salt, Pepper, Celery salt, Celery stick, Rim a tall glass with salt and fill with ice. Add vodka, fill the glass with Clamato juice, and add Worcestershire sauce, Tabasco, salt, and pepper. Garnish with a celery stick and you have a Ceasar. Here you go....

We have been talking about two types of mutual funds which are equity funds and index funds. There are other types of funds.

1. **Money market funds:** These funds invest in short-term fixed income securities such as government bonds, treasury bills, bankers' acceptances, commercial paper and certificates of deposit. They are considered a safer investment offering a lower return. Most advisors will try to steer you away from these funds wanting you to be fully invested in the market. Is this right? Are they objective? Is their recommendation based on commission?

2. **Balanced funds:** These funds invest in a mix of equities and fixed income securities. They try to balance the objective of achieving higher returns against the risk of losing money. You should not buy such a fund if its MER is higher than its equity fund.

3. **Specialty funds:** These funds focus on specialized sectors such as real estate, commodities or socially responsible investing. A real estate fund can offer an opportunity to diversify but it is also an opportunity for companies to charge higher MERs. For example, the Manulife Global Real Estate fund comes with a MER of 3.3% (2013). You also have to worry that the fund may have to put a freeze on redemptions if real estate values plummet downward as it happened to Great West Life from 2008 to 2011. Can you live without your money?

4. **Fund-of-funds:** These funds invest in other funds. These funds are bad and can charge double MER. You will have the MER of the fund purchased and the MER of the fund doing the purchasing. Avoid these funds like the pest.

5. **Proprietary funds:** These are funds created by the firm the advisor represents and work for. For example, an Investor Group advisor selling the Investor Group own brand of mutual funds. NEVER buy these funds. These funds are usually more expensive. The advisor is automatically in a conflict of interest when

recommending these funds. Is the advisor being objective or has he been told by his sales director to push that fund? Why take the chance? There is no upside here to buying these funds. You are just taking an additional risk and paying more for this. There is another problem with proprietary funds. The greatest frauds have occurred with proprietary funds. This is because the manufacturer and the distributor are the same. It makes it easy to rob from Peter to pay Paul.

WARNING: BEWARE OF CLOSET MUTUAL FUNDS!
The existence of closet mutual funds demonstrates unequivocally how the financial industry only purpose is to provide the least amount of value while charging the most amount of fees. Closet mutual funds are actively managed funds in name only. It is in fact an Index fund which uses indexing instead of active management. You are however charged higher management fees for this active management that does not exist…

The fund I really want to talk about is the Income Fund. Income funds buy investments that pay a fixed rate of return like government bonds, investment-grade corporate bonds and high-yield corporate bonds. Coming back to demographics, we all want what these funds offer. We all want an income. As a result, the popularity of these funds is increasing. I believe that this type of fund will be abused and will crash in the future when greed finds a partner in speculation.

Do you know what a ponzi scheme is? A Ponzi scheme is a fraudulent scam promising high rates of return with little risk to investors. The Ponzi scheme generates returns for older investors by acquiring new investors. This scam actually yields the promised returns to earlier investors by stealing from new investors. These schemes usually collapse when new money stop coming in.

The Ponzi scheme was named for Charles Ponzi who was an Italian businessman and a con artist in the U.S. and Canada. He became known in the early 1920s as a swindler for a scheme he created to make money. He promised clients 50% to 100% return by buying discounted postal coupons of other countries. He then suggested he could redeem them at face value in the United States as a form of arbitrage. In reality, Ponzi was paying early investors using the investments of later investors. This practice is known as "robbing Peter to pay Paul." His scheme ran for over a year before it collapsed. It cost investors over $20 million.

The greatest Ponzi scheme was done by Madoff when he founded his Wall Street firm Bernard L. Madoff Investment Securities LLC in 1960. On March 12, 2009, Madoff pleaded guilty to 11 federal felonies and admitted to turning his wealth management business into a massive Ponzi scheme. The Madoff investment scandal defrauded thousands of investors of billions of dollars.

As shown by what Madoff did, Ponzi schemes always come out when there is a high demand for a particular investment fueled by unrealistic expectations. We all want income and we all want our savings to produce 10%+ income. This is the perfect recipe for a Ponzi scheme and it just a question of time before Income Funds are used in such a way.

As interest rates and dividend yields have plunged over the past 5 years, income producing investment can barely yield a 3% income. How can firms and advisors promise a higher level of income? You want 10% income; no problem! We have a way to do it. We will simply invest in riskier investments and you will be able to take the income you want without "really" taking risks.

People desperate for more income than what their capital can safely provide are drawn to this sales pitch. They are shown actual Income Funds that are paying 10% income. Mike, I am certain you don't believe in magic. So how are they able to produce 10% income? Isn't it obvious? They are able to provide above market distributions by returning the investor's own capital and calling it income.

Let's look at the Bank of Montreal Monthly High Income fund. In October, 2011, the BMO Income Fund was priced at $7.57. The distribution was 72 cents annually. The annual yield was therefore about 9.5 per cent.

Mike do you want buy this fund? Imagine 9.5% income!!! Get me some of this! No wonder why Canadians are buying it. They have invested more than $4 billion in this fund. But here is the truth.

This BMO Income Fund never made anything close to 9.5%. In fact, it barely made 3.1% after fees. How did it make up the difference in order to return 9.5%? BMO did this by giving investors their own money back. For the moment that new money flows into the fund, it will prevent the net asset value from temporarily declining. Five years later, BMO published a notice to unit holders informing them they would be slashing distribution levels by 60% to 4.2% a year. It is important to note that if BMO had continued to credit 9.5% at this point, this would have become a Ponzi scheme because BMO would have had to use the money of new investors to sustain this yield.

BMO did achieve its objective and gotten the money it wanted. By the time unit holders are aware of a decrease in income, the unit value has been eroded so much that you can't get out without suffering a substantial loss on your capital. What a scheme!!!

Let do some simple math Mike. Imagine a fund returning 7%. Now we have to add the MER. Let's assume 2.5%. The fund manager must get a return of 9.5%. Income producing assets have a yield of 3% and constitute 40% of the portfolio. Therefore they contribute 1.2% of the 9.5%. This mean the stock which is 60% of the portfolio must yield a net return of 8.3%. When you do the math, you find that the stock portfolio must grow by about 14% per year to provide the 7% distribution if no capital is to be returned. This can't happen.

This is why if you are buying an Income fund you must do this math to calculate if the amount of return expected from the stock portfolio is realistic and whether it is based instead on return of capital. If it is based on return of capital, the Income fund comes with a lot of risk.

My ninth tip is there are no free rides. Income funds will be abused and they will crash because of unrealistic expectations. If you are buying any Income funds, you have to be certain you

are the first one to get out as soon as you see the unit price starting to fall.

Now let's talk about ETF. An exchange-traded fund (ETF) is an investment designed to replicate the performance of a specified underlying index or basket of stocks. ETFs trade on the stock exchange. They can be bought and sold just as you would a common stock. ETF are considered to be a passive investment fund. Their management costs are low, as the fund manager does not need all of this costly and worthless investment research. There is no need for active trading decisions. Like mutual funds, investors don't actually own the underlying assets of the ETF. They own shares or units and are entitled to share in dividends and gains received by the fund.

Fees are the differentiator between mutual funds and ETF. For example, a typical mutual fund charges a 2.5% MER. As we have seen, this reduces your mutual fund returns. ETFs, on the other hand, can have a MER averaging around 1% and can go as low as .5%. The low MER of the ETF does not typically include advice. If you want advice, you'll have to pay more and the cost will vary depending on what is agreed between you and the advisor. This is a great advantage. Why would you let the fund determine the cost and value of the advice you will receive? If the mutual fund pays the commission, the loyalty of the advisor is to the firm or mutual fund. If you pay the fee for the advice, you determine the cost and the value of the advice that you will receive. The advisor will have a fiduciary duty that he will owe you. There will be a contract between you and the advisor. It is a no brainer. If you don't need advice, you buy an ETF. If you need advice, you buy an ETF and negotiate a contract with an advisor that will determine what will be the responsibilities of the advisor and the cost of the services that must be provided to you. If those services are not provided, the advisor has committed a breach of contract.

Why are we not doing this Mike? Why are we still buying regular mutual funds from advisors who are not qualified to be advisors and are truly only salesmen?

We, as Canadians, have been brainwashed to go with what's

comfortable and to go with what is easy no matter the price. We are priced insensitive and this is why we always pay more than any other nations for the services we receive. We are part of the problem and this will not change until we become part of the solution. We have to demand better products and we have to stop rewarding those who provide no or little value. If we continue to buy mutual funds with high MER that provide lower returns, why would the financial industry change when this generates the most profits.

Mike, would you be surprised to know that only five mutual funds out of 100 beat an ETF?

The sales of mutual funds are sustained from the generous payouts that are made to advisors who are just glorified salesmen. It's the fuel for the growth of mutual funds sales. There are hundreds of thousands of advisors and they are paid from our assets! This is why the sales of ETF are not as successful as it should be despite being the ideal investment. This is amazing considering that ETF are so much simpler than mutual funds. ETF are easier to understand, monitor, and much cheaper. They consistently outperform mutual funds.

Unfortunately we have been brainwashed on relying on investment advisors and financial institutions for investment advice. We are not told about ETF. Mutual funds are just too profitable for these advisors to stop selling them even if ETFs might be the better investment for our savings.

The proof is in the pudding as they say. If actively managed mutual funds did better than index linked ETFs, then we could make an argument in their favor. This is not the case. Let's look at the RBC Canadian Equity Fund which has about $5 billion in assets and the Investors Canadian Large Cap Fund which has $2 billion in assets. We can compare these funds to an ETF that invest in the same underlying assets. This would reveal that the RBC fund underperformed the ETF every year. The Investors fund underperformed every year except for one. This evidence speaks for itself.

We have one last big debate to address. Is it better to invest in actively managed portfolios and pay the higher fees or in passive index-tracking ETFs with lower fees? Well this is the wrong question to ask. Who says you can't actively manage your exposure to ETF. After I have discussed everything about investing and not losing money, I will reveal how you should be investing in order to not lose any money. Not losing money is the only way to meet your retirement goals.

So don't believe those who are trying to tell you that the vast majority of investors, when left to their own devices, will do the wrong thing. It is not true that we are condemned to buy at the wrong time and sell at the wrong time. Commissioned Advisors rarely offer rational advice. Instead they play on our emotions and they become a source of bad information fueled by conflicts of interest.

My tenth tip is to always look at cost when buying an investment since it is the most important determinant of what your investment will do. If you need an advisor; hire this advisor yourself. This advisor should never be paid by the mutual fund or institution you are buying the investment from. Conflict of interest can only result in you losing money.

8 LEVERAGING: THE DOORWAY TO LOSING YOUR MONEY

When financial advice is fueled by a conflict of interest such as leveraging, the only possible guaranteed result is that you will lose your money... (The Poor Bartender)

Mike I could make the topic of leveraging very short. "Don't do it. Never!" But like so many people you would just dismiss my warning. Greed is such a powerful force.

Remember how the financial industry heavily promotes the "Buy and Hold" strategy. One argument used to promote this strategy is that the average person like you and me do not have the ability to actively manage their investments. Driven by emotions, we are doomed to buy high and sell low. The same financial industry is also heavily promoting the idea of leveraging to achieve greater returns. Suddenly our lack of emotional control disappears. Magically, we become rational enough to handle leveraging. Somehow we will not get out of the leveraging arrangement when our investment crashes while our loan continues to grow. It must be nice to work both sides of the street when you consider that leveraging is often referred as the "emotional bomb".

First I'll make you a drink Mike. I've decided on the Cosmopolitan. Like leveraging, there are a lot of contradictory claims surrounding this drink. Who created it? Was it created in the 1930s where it appears in the guide "Pioneers of Mixing at Elite Bars 1903-

1933"? It was then based on Gin instead of Vodka. Was it instead created by Cheryl Cook of the Strand Restaurant in South Beach, Florida? She said she created this drink as a substitute to the Martini that everyone was ordering. She created the Cosmo to be more palatable while being nice to the eyes.

Another important person involved in the creation of the Cosmopolitan was Melissa Huffsmith of Manhattan. While working at The Odeon in 1987/1988, her friend Patrick Mullen tasted a version of the drink in Miami. She then developed a slightly different version using Absolute Citron, Cointreau and fresh-squeezed lime juice. John Caine is also mentioned when talking about this drink. He is the owner of several popular bars in San Francisco and a cosmopolitan expert. He partially credits the upsurge in cocktails during the 1970s to the Cosmo being served at fern bars. He is credited with bringing the Cosmo west from Cleveland.

If making the Cosmo popular is the determinant factor as to whom we credit the existence of this drink, maybe we should attribute the drink to Sarah Jessica Parker. The Cosmo was popularized among young women by its frequent mentions on the television program Sex and the City. Sarah Jessica Parker acting as Carrie Bradshaw commonly ordered the drink when out with her girlfriends.

What is a true Cosmo? There are so many versions. I used the version closed to the classic version which is 1 1/2 ounces citrus vodka, 1/2 ounce Cointreau or other triple sec, 3/4 ounce chilled cranberry juice, 1/2 ounce fresh lime juice, 1/2 teaspoon Simple Syrup and 1 lemon twist, for garnish.

I hope you'll enjoy this drink while we dig in the worst money making concept devised and promoted by the financial industry. This concept is leveraging.

You do not get yourself out of a hole by digging a bigger hole. You don't build investments to retire on by using leveraging. They say that 46% of high net worth clients used leveraging as an investment strategy. They use good debt in order to invest in things like businesses, real estate or the stock market, which generally increase in value over time. The argument is therefore that we should do like the wealthy are doing. Leveraging should not be restricted to only those who have lots of money. Sounds a lot like investing like Buffet, right?

Again investing for income is different than investing for growth. While leveraging is an opportunity for growth, it represents a risk for income; a risk that you and me cannot take.

I remember attending a 2001 presentation sponsored by Sun Life made by the guru of leveraging. His name was Talbot Stevens. He was hired by banks, mutual funds and insurance companies to convince us that leveraging was the answer to our retirement problems. It was even better than RRSPs. I still have the press release he wrote about this.

Conservative Leverage Even Better Than RRSPs

New Cut in Capital Gains Taxes Makes Strategy Better
While RRSPs are one of the best investment strategies, most Canadians can produce even more retirement income by borrowing to invest outside of RRSPs.

"Now that only 50% of capital gains are taxable, the poorly understood approach of leveraging or borrowing to invest can be an even better retirement savings strategy than RRSPs," says Talbot Stevens, financial educator and author of the new bestselling booklet Dispelling the Myths of Borrowing to Invest.

"Leveraging has always been used by the wealthy", says Stevens. "Now, more middle-income Canadians are starting to realize how tax-effective it can be to borrow to invest in equity investments outside of RRSPs"

When you borrow to invest outside of RRSPs, the interest expense is generally tax-deductible, and produces the same tax savings as an RRSP contribution. RRSP dollars are 100% taxable when withdrawn. But when you borrow for equity investments, much of your returns are in the form of capital gains which are only 50% taxable.

Stevens points out that an overlooked benefit of equity funds is that the tax on capital gains is deferred until you, or your fund manager, sells. This means that a tax-efficient equity fund can provide almost the same tax deferral benefit as RRSPs. When you combine this with the fact that the interest expense produces the same tax deduction as an RRSP contribution and that only half of the gains are taxable, it is easy to see how leverage can be better.

Stevens provides an example using conservative assumptions to illustrate. Both Randy and Linda are 45 year-old baby boomers in the 40% tax bracket and invest $4,000 a year, a little less than the average RRSP contribution. They both invest for 20 years, averaging 9% equity fund returns and will retire in the 40% tax bracket.

Linda, the leveraged investor, uses her cashflow to pay 9% interest on a $44,444 investment loan. Both want their retirement income to last 20 years, from age 65 to 85.

Using RRSPs, Randy, produces an annual retirement income of $13,450 after-tax from age 65 to 85. Using leverage, Linda ends up with a 20-year after-tax income of $14,490. In this case, leveraging produces an extra $1,000 a year during her retirement, after-tax. This is assuming conservative 9% annual returns that just match the cost of borrowing, while long-term global equity fund returns have averaged closer to 12%.

If investment returns are 12%, the leveraged investor ends up with 37% more after-tax retirement income than produced with RRSPs. Linda has an after-tax income of $31,680 per year, while Randy has $23,150.

With the use of margin accounts at record levels, Talbot Stevens' booklet is timely for investors trying to understand when it makes sense to borrow outside of RRSPs, or to use a loan to catch-up on unused RRSP contribution room. (Press release by Talbot Stevens who is a financial educator, industry consultant)

What a pile of crap! Leveraging better than RRSPs! Can you believe Mike that this guy was allowed to promote this poisonous message? What does that tell you about Sun Life? It's the cyanide pill for your retirement. I was lucky. I didn't buy into the concept. At the time I did not know why. I did not have the same knowledge I have today. It just sounded very fishy.

Now I know today why I felt that way. First observe the words "assuming conservative 9% annual returns". Since we are talking about unregistered funds, the true MER of these funds because of taxable distributions is around 4.5%. To get 9%, the funds must earn 13% to 14% every year for 20 years. You call this conservative? Find me a fund which provided this return. Can you Mike? Talbot even tries to put more upside to the leveraging strategy by quoting a 12% return which pushes what the fund must earn between 16% and 17%.

The second problem is the loan rate. Talbot uses a loan rate of 9%. Sounds conservative compared to a loan rate of 6%. However deductibility of interest on the loan is used to reduce the loan rate. Assuming the tax rate is 50%, the net loan rate is 4.5%. The difference in interest rate is now 1.5% and not 3% for a loan rate of 9% versus 6% investment rate. The higher the loan rate the greater the impact of the interest deductibility will be. This can be used to convince someone this is a conservative assumption. "After all we are using a high loan rate!!!" However when interest is a tax deduction, a high loan rate becomes an aggressive assumption.

Find me someone who understands this.

There is also no talk or provision for volatility. The fund has to earn 13% every year for the next 20 years. I love to show volatility this way. Let's assume the fund historic high is 25% and historic low -25%. Assuming 13%, your maximum gain is 12% (25%-13%) and your maximum loss is 38% (25% + 13%). This is a 3 to 1 loss to gain ratio. If you were to earn -25% in the first year, it will take you 3 years at +25% to make up that loss in order to achieve THAT CONSERVATIVE and constant rate of return of 13%. That's how volatility can destroy you when you assume a ridiculous CONSTANT rate of return.

This is why everyone who entered into a leveraging arrangement using mutual funds lost money unless they used market timing to take advantage of short term swings in the market. As a long term strategy, to increase your investments needed for retirement, you were guaranteed to lose most of your money.

As soon as an advisor proposes leveraging, he is in a conflict of interest. The advisor will increase his commission substantially. The advisor is guaranteed to make a lot of money if you buy into leveraging while you take all of the risks while you are guaranteed to lose money. Does that sound good to you?

Let me mention Ray and Dawn-Marie Brown who never played the markets but, as they moved towards retirement, they made the mistake of consulting a financial advisor. The advisor quickly saw the opportunity to make some commission and convinced them to borrow $200,000 under the excuse that it was a great way to secure a better retirement.

Instead, they have found that their investments were not growing while their debt was. They were now more than $30,000 in debt. This was after borrowing money on a line of credit to repay the leveraged loan. These people were 74 and 72 years old. Do you think they could afford to burn through virtually all their money in their Registered Retirement Income Fund in order to pay the interest on their loan while desperately looking at their declining assets?

It is only after all this happened that they realize their advisor had lied by putting on their application that their knowledge about investing was excellent and that they were ready and willing to take on high risk when investing.

To add to the injury, they had to pay a 3%, or $5,000, fee to sell their investment to pay off the loan.

The Browns dealt with an advisor at Quadrus Investment Services Ltd., a mutual fund dealer affiliated with London Life and Great-West Life.

Another scoundrel was former financial advisor, John Alexander Allen who represented Global Maxfin Investments Inc. of Toronto and Keybase Financial Group Inc. of Markham, Ont. He was accused of negligence and breach of contract for the investment losses of a Trenton, Ontario woman

The victim Grace Weatherbie met Allen in 2005. She was 47 years old and only earning $20,000. Worst she was working part time. Do you think she had any investment experience? Where would she get that experience making $20,000? Allen put her into a leveraging arrangement and the loan grew to $375,000 by the end of 2007.

As expected the mutual funds purchased did not increase in value. They decreased in value. This is what happens when we leverage for the purpose of building up our retirement.

LEVERAGING BY TAKING A LOAN AGAINST YOUR HOME IS THE DEFINITON OF INSANITY.

The worst type of leveraging is to borrow against your house to buy mutual funds. With the rise of home prices, advisors were quick in seeing the opportunity to make money. They started to tell their clients to tap into a home equity line of credit. Such advisors are very persuasive. They will say and do anything to get their fat commission.

My advice to you is simple. You never leverage or borrow against your home to buy mutual funds. Your home is a great asset and provides a great diversification. Remember how I told you that because of demographics, investment opportunities are few. Your home is one of these investment opportunities and it is impacted positively by demographics. This is why home prices are going up. Why would you borrow against your home, and reinvest in the market which now means you are putting your investments in only one kind of asset. The risk is too high. If the equity market crashes you are doomed; if the real estate market crashes you are doomed when you would been able to ride out the storm if you had not used leveraging.

Diversifying investment is the hardest thing to achieve. Why would you destroy one of the only assets that allow you to diversify by leveraging your home?

The best method to unlock home equity is to scale down. If your house is worth $500,000; selling it to buy a home worth $300,000 and invest the $200,000 is the only way to not lose money. You however invest this money into something guaranteed and forget all about it until retirement. Don't let a greedy advisor convince you to bet this money in the market. You'll lose.

If you don't want to sell your home and still want to unlock equity; then borrow against it but select an investment that will protect you by providing more diversification like an income property. Agricultural lands are also a good investment since they will not decrease in value. Earth population is increasing and we can't feed everyone. What do you think will happen to the value of agricultural lands? A cottage on the water if it is not overpriced is a good idea. If it can be rented, it can become a great income opportunity. However financial advisors don't make commissions out of these choices. This is why they won't talk about it.

Just this week, the Ontario Securities Commission issued a warning to investors about the risks of leveraged investing. They stated exactly what I am now telling you now. Leveraging increases your investment risk; and you're on the hook to pay off your loan even if your investments tank. Is that clear enough?

The number of complaints about leveraging is rising. There were 30 complaints on leveraging in 2010 versus 16 in 2009 for Ontario alone. This is only what is reported. Most of the time, victims feel too much shame and don't make a complaint; anyway making a complaint rarely result in the victim getting compensated for their losses. A report by the New Brunswick Securities Commission on leverage practices found that there was a high correlation between leveraged investing, unsuitable investments and losses to consumers. The report found that in 68 percent of cases, the use of leverage was aggressive and were in a loss position. 68%!!! Mike, what other evidence do you need to have to see that leveraging is bad?

9 THE TRUTH ABOUT SEGREGATED FUNDS

The history of segregated funds is the smoking gun, providing conclusive evidence, that financial advisors and in particular mutual fund advisors do not provide advice for our benefit but instead provide advice based on their license which determines what they can sell and make commission on. This goes against our best interest. (The Poor Bartender)

Today, Mike I wish I was not working so I could enjoy a drink with you. This is how disturbing my next topic is. I need a drink also… but I never drink on the job. Let's lubricate these brain cells of yours…

I'm going to make a Rusty Nail. The history of this drink is tied to the Prohibition. Drambuie and other spirits could no longer legally enter United States. Ships would have to dump their cargo offshore just beyond U.S. waters. Smugglers would row out and bring the liqueur back ashore. It was then mixed with whatever they had on hand to make it more palatable. The exact origin of this drink is unclear. Some credits F. Benniman for this drink he created for the British Industries Fair trade show, which took place in 1937. His drink was based on a 3 to 1 ratio of scotch to Drambuie. For decades, the Rusty Nail was a hot cocktail. By the late 1960s, watering holes in New Orleans and New York were serving the drink, and "have you tried a Rusty Nail?" was a common thing to say. The Rat Pack and this means Frank Sinatra were enamored with this drink, which may have been responsible for its wide appeal during these years. The Rusty Nail has evolved and is now made of 1.5 oz of Scotch, .75 oz Drambuie, Lemon twist and ice. You pour these ingredients into the glass and just stir well.

Now we are ready to talk about segregated funds. Segregated (or seg) funds are an investment product sold by life insurance companies. They are individual insurance contracts that invest in one or more underlying assets. They are very much like a mutual fund. For insurance to be able to sell these funds, the law requires that they have an insurance component. The insurance component of the seg funds is called a guarantee. There are three types of guarantee.

The first guarantee is the guarantee of capital. It works this way. The guarantee has a maturity date. It is usually 10 years away. You deposit $100,000 and in 10 years, you are guaranteed at maturity to have $100,000. You can reset the guarantee if the market goes up and lock in the higher value of the market. For example, if the value of your fund is now $125,000 you can guarantee this amount. There is a catch however. This also resets the maturity date of the guarantee to a new 10 year period.

This capital guarantee cost money. Usually it will cost between .75% and 1% of your asset value. This means the MER of the seg fund is higher than the MER of the mutual fund by at least that amount. This higher MER represented the perfect opportunity for the mutual fund industry to discredit this product. Mutual fund sales representatives all said the same thing: "Why pay for this guarantee when it is proven that over a period of 10 years you will never lose any of your capital." I can tell you these mutual fund salesmen were pretty certain of themselves. It's an easy thing to say when it is not your money on the line.

They were all wrong! In fact, the guarantee came into play often because of the high volatility of the market. Worst, it was discovered that what was presented as being expensive was in fact a bargain. The insurance industry had priced this guarantee too low.

The evidence is all there for anyone to see. This guarantee is not available anymore.

As I said, mutual fund salesmen discouraged their clients from using this product not because it was not good but because they could not sell it and they could not make commissions off it. A lot of people lost a lot of money because of this. It is shameful!

Who should have bought this type of seg funds? Let me tell you a story Mike. Remember Robert the insurance agent in the feud; well one day he asked if he could make an appointment with me to discuss my retirement. I said yes. What did I have to lose? Anyway he analyzed my investments and did a KYC which is an analysis of the risk I could take. Not surprisingly, since I do not like to lose money, my preferred asset allocation was a balanced type of fund. Robert then tried to convince me to switch to a seg fund. He talked about the guarantee of 100% on the capital and how I could not lose my initial investment.

"One moment," I said. "You understand that by investing in a balanced fund, I am self insuring the risk I can take. You agree that if the market is bullish, the fact that I invested in a balanced fund will result in less returns which represents the cost of self insuring. Why would I buy a second insurance for a risk which I am already paying to manage? Don't get me wrong. I love the guarantee. I think it is great because now I can increase the risk I can take. Instead of investing in a balanced fund, I would be ok in investing fully in equity because of this guarantee. Basically instead of self insurance, I am willing to cede this risk to the insurer in the hope of making a greater return by investing 100% in equity versus a balanced fund."

"But you can't do this," answered Robert. "It is against compliance for me to put you into a fund which has a higher risk than you can take."

"Robert, this assessment was based on me not wanting to lose my initial capital. If I insure this risk and I can't lose my initial capital because of the insurance, I need to take advantage of this. I need a potential payoff that would be greater than the cost of this guarantee, right? If I don't do this it's like buying CHMC mortgage insurance which allows me to borrow up to 95% of the value of a house but still borrow 75% of this value which can be done without insurance. Who would do this?

We had a big discussion about this. It seems the industry and regulators don't understand insurance. Even if the risk is insured, an advisor cannot sell you a product with a risk that you can't take even if you are not taking that risk anymore because it is insured.

I did not buy the segregated funds. It's too bad because I liked the product.

Now the segregated funds with the 100% guarantee are not available anymore. It's not surprising. The insurance industry was not able to defend and successfully sell this product when it was under priced. How could they sell it when it would now be correctly priced at a much higher price? Instead they reduced the guarantee to 75% and you now have the opportunity to lose 25% of your initial capital before the insurance kicks in. To close the topic on the capital guarantee here are some tips for you:

Tip eleven: Understand that a capital guarantee of 75% is worth nothing. As a result, if you buy a segregated fund with this guarantee, the MER of the segregated fund should be the same as the equivalent mutual fund you could buy.

If you have purchased a segregated fund with a 100% guarantee, it is important to know:

Tip twelve: Monitor the guarantee in order to not pay for insurance you don't need. For example, the value of the seg fund is $150,000 and the guarantee is $100,000. Normally you would reset to $150,000. However if you can't because your retirement date is less than 10 years away, then you have to decide whether it is worthwhile to get out and move to something with less risk in order to protect and self insure the $150,000. Why would stay in the seg fund and pay for insurance that does not protect you anymore? If the guarantee was worth $150,000 and the fund was worth $100,000 then it would be entirely different.

Tip thirteen: Never stay in a seg fund with a guarantee of

100% if you have moved from a RRSP to a RRIF. You will be paying for insurance that will become worthless. Guarantees, when withdrawals are made, are reduced on a prorata basis. For example, the value of your fund is $100,000 and the guarantee is $150,000. You make a $10,000 withdrawal. This is 10% of the value of your fund. This means the guarantee will be reduced by 10% which is $15,000. This decrease is 150% more than your RRIF withdrawal. As a result, the value of your guarantee will decrease faster than the value of your fund. It is just a question of a short period of time before the guarantee become lower than the value of your RRIF. Why would you keep this sort of guarantee? Why would you pay an MER for it?

Mike we are done with the guarantee of capital. There is another guarantee offered by seg funds which is called the death benefit guarantee. This type of guarantee either insures 100% of your initial capital or the value of the fund if there was a reset. If you die, the value of this guarantee is paid to the designated beneficiary. I like this guarantee. You can't predict when you will die. If you die in a bear market and you had a spouse who also relied on the income of your investment, insuring the value of your fund is important. The important question is what is the cost of this guarantee in relation to its value? I believe you should not accept to pay more than 25 basis points for this guarantee. If your choice is a mutual fund with a MER of 1.5% and you want to look at a seg fund with this guarantee, its MER should not be higher than 1.75%. This is based on the assumption that you are healthy. If you are not insurable because your life expectancy is lower than the normal, then the death benefit guarantee offers a lot of value since it is not based on the evaluation of your health.

We are almost done Mike! The last guarantee offered by seg funds is a guarantee of income. This guarantee came late to Canada. It was brought from the U.S.A. by Manulife. Manulife demonstrated that saving money for producing a future income was the hardest thing to do when volatility is involved. In fact, it is mathematically proven that volatility can reduce you wealth and therefore your income by as much as 50% even if you achieve the rate of return you were targeting.

Remember one thing. All of the retirement plans you see are based on a constant rate of return. Basically advisors censor volatility. I suppose it makes everything clean, neat and tidy. But then the real world happens and volatility dirties everything up. How your money will grow over 20 years for example, will not only be based on the rate of return over 20 years but also on the sequence of rate of returns. This is almost impossible to manage and this is why advisors prefer to forget about it knowing that their clients would be none the wiser.

What if there was a way to manage this volatility without having to transfer your investment into something that is less volatile. This is what the income guarantee does. With the income guarantee, you know exactly what will be your minimum level of income for your entire life. Basically the guarantee will give you an income of 5% of your deposits or 5% of the market value of your investment if there was a reset. Let's assume you put in $100,000 into this type of seg fund and the market crashes. Your fund is now worth only $70,000. You could elect to take your guaranteed income of $5,000 based on $100,000 and not $70,000.

Again this type of guarantee is a form of insurance. Insurance will always have a cost. The cost of this guarantee is about 75 basis points. Please note that the .75% is applied against the value of the guarantee and not the value of your fund.

Was this a good product and guarantee? Well it is certainly not for everyone. Considering how bad volatility is, I believe a good part of the population should have considered this product or this form of insurance. But again the mutual fund advisors went on the attack by focusing on the cost of the product. Again they were wrong. Again all of the mutual fund industry provided the wrong advice to Canadians because they could not sell this seg fund product.

We learned later that this guarantee was underpriced; extremely underpriced. It was so underpriced that it could have bankrupted Manulife. Maybe the Mutual Fund industry did a favor to the insurance industry. If everyone had realized how this product was a bargain and how crazy it was to introduce it at the height of the market allowing you to lock in an income guarantee based on the TSX at 15,000, it would have bankrupted companies such as Manulife.

Today segregated funds with this income guarantee cost the same but the features of the guarantee are less competitive. They offer a lot less value. So you are getting a lot less for your money. It is just so sad that Canadians did not take advantage of this opportunity because of the false information provided by mutual fund advisors.

Should you buy this product today? What I suggest to you is that since the seg funds with the income guarantee provide a lot less value today because of product changes, you have to ensure to maximize its potential. One of the problems in maximizing the value of this product is the advice gap. The advice gap represents the gap between the knowledge an advisor has and the knowledge he needs to effectively manage a product he has sold. Seg funds with this type of guarantee are extremely complex. Very complex mathematics is required to project or model the future behavior of these products. Advisors simply don't have this knowledge. As a result, this is not a product you should normally consider unless the market is very bullish at the time of purchase.

For example, you could use this product to lock in your market gains. Let's assume you are approaching retirement and the market is hot as it was in 2008 when it was at 15,000. You have to protect this gain. You could go out of the market and invest in something that is guaranteed or you could stay in the market but you get some insurance by buying this income guarantee offered by these seg funds. Even if the market goes down, the seg funds have a feature where it will increase this guarantee by 5% every year for the next 10 to 15 years if you don't do any withdrawals. Having a guarantee locked in when the market was at 15000 with the guarantee increasing by 5% every year, this would be worth a lot of money.

Tip fourteen: "Treat guarantees of segregated funds as insurance. Understand that insurance has a cost. Understand that the purpose of insurance is to insure an unlikely event. In

most cases, it will not be used. Does this make insurance bad? No, since it is a necessity. The question is: do you need it? The next question is: does it provide enough value for the cost? You only win with insurance if the worst happens. This is the value of insurance. Since you do not want the worst to happen, you have to accept that insurance will reduce your future income as a cost. Finally, compare the cost of this insurance to the cost of a self insured strategy you can use to mitigate risk. Managing risk will always cost money."

10 RRIF AND INCOME

Retirement is like a blanket. You can pull on the blanket as much as you want; it won't get any bigger. The only result will be to uncover another part of the bed. (The Poor Bartender)

Well Mike we did it! We went through the subject of mutual funds/segregated funds and it was not an easy task. My next topic is the Registered Retirement Income Fund. A registered retirement income fund (RRIF) is an arrangement between you and a carrier which can be an insurance company, a trust company or a bank to purchase a product registered with the government allowing for tax deferral until you retire and take an income. You transfer property to the carrier in your RRIF from an RRSP, a PRPP, an RPP, an SPP, or from another RRIF. The carrier must pay you at least the minimum income as legislated by the government. This income is taxable.

A RRIF is therefore a tax-deferred retirement plan under Canadian tax law. Most Canadians use a RRIF to generate income from the savings accumulated under our Registered Retirement Savings Plan (RRSP). We can convert a RRSP into an RRIF anytime but we have to do it before reaching 71 of age. Before the end of the year in which we turn 71, it is mandatory to either withdraw all funds from a RRSP plan or convert the RRSP to a RRIF or life annuity. If the funds are simply withdrawn from a RRSP, the entire amount is fully taxable as ordinary income. We can however partly defer this taxation by transferring investments from a RRSP into a RRIF.

This is a RRIF in a nutshell. This kind of information makes me thirsty. Let me get you a Stinger. The Stinger has always been considered a society drink the same way a RRIF is considered for better or worse a society saving vehicle.

The origin of the Stinger cocktail is very obscure. Some say it was created to disguise the taste of alcohol during prohibition. A bit like the RRIF hides the problem of pension in the retirement age… Others argue this is not the case, as the Stinger existed before prohibition and was a very popular drink. It is listed in the Tom Bullock's 1917 Ideal Bartender guide. It is the same thing with the RRIF. It was sold to the Canadian public as a substitute to a pension plan. An individual not having access to a pension plan would be on the same footing basis to those who have a pension plan by being able to invest in a RRSP which can then be converted to a RRIF. This is far from the truth… and we will see why… but coming back to the Stinger…

As for most drinks, it is not important to know who created the Stinger but who made it popular. This is what counts. This drink is associated with Reginald Vanderbitl who was a millionaire equestrian and father of Gloria who was an artist, actress and who developed the concept of designer jeans. Sometime in the early 1920s, Reginald Vanderbilt who believed religiously in the ritual of cocktail hour was known for making up Stingers behind the bar in his home. His bar looked like the bar in the William the Conqueror tavern in Normandy.

A Stinger is made with 2 1/4 ounces of brandy and 3/4 ounce crème de menthe. You shake well with cracked ice then strain into a chilled cocktail glass. With this drink in hand, we are equipped to handle one of the most challenging tasks associated with retirement. How do you effectively go from wealth accumulation to income generation? How do you produce income from assets without destroying the wealth you have built over the years with the consequence of outliving your assets? Most people do not even consider these questions when retiring and as a result they lose tons of money. It is proven that most people lose money during this transition. You better have a plan to deal specifically with this problem. You can't make up a plan at the last minute…

Do you know Mike that there are serious flaws in the design of the RRIF that makes it impossible for this product to provide us a retirement income to age 100? Basically, the government has set us up to fail. Someone who has a defined benefit pension plan such as our politicians (nothing but the best for them) does not have to worry about outliving his income. For the regular person who does not have a pension because he is self employed, work for a small employer or live and work in a rural area, well this person is stuck in using a RRIF that was designed to disappear by age 90. Is this fair?

The first flaw was with the RRIF minimum withdrawals. You know that when you transfer a RRSP into a RRIF you are forced to take out a minimum withdrawal every year. The minimum withdrawals are calculated based on rates established by the government. The thing is that these minimum withdrawals were calculated based on old life expectancies with the government believing you were pretty much dead by age 90.

As a result, by just taking the minimum out of the RRIF, it was guaranteed that you were going to be out of money between age 90 and 95. This was not a choice. This was a guaranteed outcome of the RRIF. When the government forces you to take between 15 to 20% out of your RRIF, how long do you think your assets are going to last? If you get a good investment return…maybe 5 years. If you are invested in the market and you are forced to take out 20% and the market loses 20% of its value, in one year, you are losing more than 40% of your retirement assets. These assets are gone. It is not sustainable…

Now the government has finally seen the light… 40 years too late. It has reduced these minimums by about 2%. For example, at age 71, instead of being forced to withdraw 7.38%, you are now forced to withdraw 5.2%. For every $100,000 of RRIF this is $2,100 less withdrawal for that year. However for this to work, you have to be able to live on $2,100 less a year for every $100,000 of RRIF you have. I could not and most Canadians can't.

Most Canadians who don't have a pension plan will outlive their income. But they can rest easy knowing that their politicians are well looked after. These politicians have a pension plan which will provide them with a guaranteed income no matter how long they live. This will give ample time for these politicians to criticize us for not having saved enough money for retirement...

Remember this segregated fund we discussed earlier which had an income guarantee? Well, I was talking to one of my friend who has a RRIF with Manulife. He bought this kind of segregated fund with the income guarantee. He was telling me how the change to the RRIF minimums impacted him. One of his RRIF was a Manulife Income Plus and yes, you can in fact have multiple RRIF. This is one of the thing people don't understand very well.

As I was saying, he was taking the RRIF minimum in order to not reduce his income guarantee. This RRIF minimum was used to pay his car loan which was a payment of $500 monthly. This year, his RRIF withdrawal was reduced by more than $100 monthly because of the change and decrease to the RRIF minimums. His RRIF withdrawal did not cover his car loan anymore. He was short by $1,200 annually. He was left with the choice of either increasing his RRIF withdrawal back to what it was before. However, since his new payment would be above the RRIF minimum, this payment would reduce his guarantee. This meant, by increasing his RRIF withdrawal above the minimum, he would be destroying his guarantee. You have to remember; he paid a lot of money for this guarantee over the years. As a result, he could not do this and he needed another source of income to make the difference. He certainly did not have the option of reducing his car loan by $100 each month.

The consequence of the RRIF changes is that by reducing the legislated RRIF minimums, it has increased the importance of the RRIF PERSONAL minimums. RRIF changes can now only provide a retirement income for life if you take the minimum allowed. If you need more income, the government's fix of reducing the minimums provides no value to you. You are still going to run out of money. It may sound complicated but this is where a rule of thumb can be handy to show the real face and impact of these changes. This rule of thumb is the Rule of 5.

What is this Rule of 5?

The rule of 5 states that if a retiree wants a retirement to age 100 based on the current legislated RRIF minimum withdrawals, assuming an earned rate of return of 5%, his personal minimum cannot be higher than 5%. For example, for a $100,000 RRIF, his personal minimum income cannot be higher than $5,000. No problem you state since at age 71, the minimum RRIF withdrawal is 5.28%. So on a $100,000 RRIF, the government will force him to take out $5,280. Since the personal minimum is below the legislated minimum, by taking out the legislated minimum, the RRIF should provide an income for life.

This is partly true until the RRIF balance become low enough to have an impact. What if the RRIF was now worth $50,000 and the minimum withdrawal was 7.08% at age 81. The legislated minimum would be about $3,500 to have an income for life. However his personal minimum is $5,000. Since this $5,000 is what he needs to survive, he has a difficult choice to make. Either he chooses to survive on a lower income, lower by $1,500, or he chooses an income of $5,000 which will mean that he will outlive his assets. What do you choose?

Based on the Rule of 5, if you wanted a $40,000 minimum personal income to age 100, a RRIF of $800,000 would be required. How many Canadians have an $800,000 RRIF versus those who want a $40,000 income? I think there is a shit load of people wanting a $40,000 income versus those who will have $800,000... Retirement planning for most Canadians is out of whack and nobody is talking about it or planning for it...

Mike, I don't have an $800,000 RRIF either but I need an income of $40,000. What I am going to do? Am I doomed?

On top of this, the 5% earned rate of return is not conservative. This is a very aggressive rate of return as the only mean to achieve this rate of return is to take some risk. Risky investments come with high Management Expense Ratio. To meet your plan, the investment gross return would have to be 8% every single year to age 100. You are taking risks but it is not factored into the retirement plan…

The problem is that advisors are so focus on building wealth that they have no idea on how to build income. Building income is entirely different than building wealth. More wealth does not necessarily translate into more income. Most advisors have no idea about how to manage "TRANSITIONS" and most wealth losses are created during "TRANSITIONS"

What are transitions? Transitions are the moment when money gets into an investment and out of an investment on a periodical basis.

It seems to me that advisors are in denial or are totally ignorant of what they have to do. While everybody talks about the retirement crisis fueled by a retirement saving shortfall, many advisors are still denying for example that reverse mortgages will play an important role at retirement or during retirement. In fact, many retirement choices are not disclosed and included in retirement planning. Is this because these choices don't generate commissions?

Mike, I am going back to my original question? What am I going to do in order to create an income? If I was to attempt answering this question I have to look at my choices.

A great choice would be annuities. Even if interest rates are low, annuities still play an important role in retirement. Low interest rates have not rendered this product worthless. You certainly should invest less in this product but it still provides a great "INCOME" foundation to build upon. Mike, I know you don't like numbers but we have to look at some numbers here. Let's say you are age 71 and you have a $100,000 RRIF. To get a life income, you can only take out the minimum RRIF and this is 5.28% or $5,280. Right from the start with an annuity you would get a $7,800 GUARANTEED income FOR LIFE (note: June 2016 annuity quote). It is only at age 92, that the RRIF minimum income of $7,995 would become greater than the annuity income. But this won't last forever. It will only last to age 95 and then the RRIF income would drop below the annuity income.

Here is the catch with the RRIF. Our RRIF calculations are based on a 5% earned rate of return. Again where are you going to find an investment that will yield a 5% net return? A Guaranteed Investment certificate? I don't think so. Bonds? I don't think so. The only way to get this return is to take some risk and invest into equity. But then you are faced with MERs and the return you need is not 5% anymore; it will be 7.5% to 8% when you add the MER of 2.5% to 3%. What is your chance of earning a sequence of changing, year to year rates of return, which will yield an income similar to the income guaranteed by the annuity?

Let's show the risk associated with this. Let's assumed you just missed the 5% net rate of return by 1%. This means you have earned an average net return of 4% instead. This is the equivalent to a gross rate return of 6.5% when the MER of 2.5% is added back in. At 4%, the RRIF income never goes above $6,500 of income. The annuity therefore beats the RRIF every single year by quite a margin. But people's mind conditioned by the financial industry is so set against annuities that people simply disregard the mathematics…

But I hear you… What if I die early? What if I take the $100,000 to buy an annuity and I die tomorrow? I would lose everything… Yes, you are right, Mike. But you know, your need is retirement and not estate planning unless you have a spouse. You can't have it all. Buying a guarantee on the annuity is not that expensive anyway. A 10 year guarantee on the annuity would reduce the annuity payment from $7,800 to $7,200. Basically this 10 year guarantee would insure 75% of your capital. The annuity with the 10 year guarantee would still be better than the RRIF if you were to earn a gross return of 6.5% (4% net). At 5% net return, the RRIF would start to be better at age 89 instead of 92.

I am not telling you to put everything in annuities but they should be used to a certain extent. However this is not happening. Advisors are not promoting it and the financial industry have brainwashed the consumers into believing that annuities are bad. Why is that?

The problem with annuities is how advisors are licensed. Many Canadians do not include an annuity in their retirement plan because their advisor is not licensed to sell this product. Therefore the advisor does not recommend this product.

On December 16, 2011, Minister of Finance Jim Flaherty announced that the government of Canada would soon introduce legislation to prevent banks from offering financial products that produce the same results as life annuities offered by insurers. Canadians need life income. Canadians need life retirement solutions. But here, you have the Canadian Finance Minister announcing that he will prohibit one of the most important financial institution involve in retirement planning from helping Canadians with this huge financial problem.

In Canada, you have to know that life annuities are treated as insurance products. Under existing legislation, banks are prohibited from undertaking the business of insurance. They can't sell insurance except for credit or mortgage insurance. Life insurers in Canada are, on the other hand, authorized to issue life annuities, but they have to maintain appropriate levels of long-term capital and reserves.

Banks are not happy about this. Canadians are not happy with this either. Find me a Canadian who needs a retirement solution which would provide him a guaranteed income to age 100 and who would be ok to find that his financial and retirement advisor at the bank can't help him with this.

It is therefore not surprising that in recent years, some Canadian banks introduced products that performed very much like life annuities. This is where is gets weird. On the excuse, that these bank annuity-like products are not subject to the same regulatory standards as life annuities sold by insurance companies, the Minister of Finance believed that the banks should not be able to provide guaranteed retirement solutions to age 100.

This is insanity pure and simple. In order to guarantee the separation of the business of banking and insurance, Flaherty introduced legislative amendments in 2012 to prohibit banks from offering such annuity-similar products. But the problem is that banks like the insurers are offering the same service to Canadians. They are offering the same retirement services. Why would a customer have to take a lot of risk to have a retirement income to age 100 because banks can't offer annuity like products while the same consumer can get access to guaranteed retirement income to age 100 if he deals with an insurer? How is he supposed to know this?

As a result of this, banks representatives will focus on greed meaning the creation of more wealth by convincing Canadians to take more risk than they should. This is the only way these bank representatives passing themselves as financial advisors will be able to make a sale and get their commission. When this blows up and Canadians run out of income, who will be blamed? Not the politicians who created this evil system. By the way, these politicians will be retired happy enjoying a life retirement income guaranteed by a very generous pension plan.

The next investment choice I have is a segregated fund with an income guarantee.

I have to say that I am very concerned with these segregated funds. I am concerned with the lack of knowledge shown by advisors, lack of tools to manage the guarantees and lack of disclosure surrounding these guarantees.

I am particularly concerned with the segregated funds where the income guarantee is reduced by a RRIF minimum withdrawal. For example, your life income guarantee is 5% on $200,000 which is $10,000. Your RRIF balance is $100,000 but the RRIF minimum is 20%. You would be required to withdraw $20,000. What would be the impact on your guarantee? Your guarantee will be reduced by $40,000. So now your life income guarantee is not 5% of $200,000 but 5% of $160,000. You just lost $2,000 of life guaranteed income which you paid for!!!

Every year this will happen with any RRIF where your legislated minimum withdrawal is more than 5% and there is no way out!!!

THIS IS A DISASTER and advisors are clueless that they are selling a worthless guarantee unless they are able to model the future behavior of this guarantee to determine its sweet spot!!!

I do not see any possibilities that the life income guarantee would survive under a RRIF. So you are going to pay .75% MER during all the accumulation part of your retirement to find out that you have purchased worthless insurance. I have studied the documents of one insurance company and this has not been disclosed ANYWHERE!!! I called this a major problem, Mike!

Another investment choice is an Income Fund:

Again we have another area of concern. Many consumers are enticed in buying an Income Fund that credits an income of 8% to 10%. Who wouldn't, right?

However, when you check the Income Fund earned rate of return, it is well below what they are giving away.

This means that what you are getting back is your capital and if this is maintained; possibly the capital of other people joining into the Income Fund. This is a Ponzi scheme and will only last until people stop buying into the fund or too much capital has been returned. Then you will have a severe income correction by more than 50%!!! Shame on an industry for promoting and selling a Ponzi scheme… This is what happens when a Finance Minister prohibits the selling of a guaranteed income product!

So truly, if I am going to survive my retirement, I am going to have to look at non-traditional sources of income.

I could look at a reverse mortgage.

The reverse mortgage will be one of the most useful tools used in retirement. It will save the retirement of countless Canadians. I strongly believe in using a reverse mortgage paid over 15 years to supplement retirement income. The question is not whether a reverse mortgage should be done; the question is when it should be done.

Advisors are amazingly absent from this decision; not being involved with reverse mortgages with many believing it is not the right option. Is it because they won't be making commissions?

What I am concerned is to see that when advisors are involved, consumers are influenced into taking a lump sum payment instead of periodical payments. This allows the advisor to invest this lump sum which will generate commissions to the advisor. This ceased to be a reverse mortgage. This becomes a leveraged investment scheme and it will only end badly for the client like any leveraged arrangements. The purpose of a reverse mortgage should be to provide a guaranteed income. You should not bet this money in the market!!!

I could also look into a Life Settlement.

First let's explain what a life settlement is. A life settlement is any arrangements where you sell your life insurance policy to a third party. When you cancel a life insurance policy, you are basically entering into a life settlement with an insurer. You are giving away the death benefit of the life insurance policy in exchange for the receipt of the cash value if it has one. If it does not have a cash value, you are selling your policy to the insurer for nothing.

There are third parties who are looking for investment opportunities that provide a stable return. Buying life insurance policies and packaging them as a form of investment provide such returns.

Why would your policy be worth anything when the insurer is telling you it is worth nothing?

This is how they do it. Imagine you need insurance and it will cost you 1 insurance dollar. This is a yearly increasing cost of insurance. Next year, the insurance will cost you 2 insurance dollars. The following year, you will have to pay 3 insurance dollars. I think you get the picture.

Now the insurance advisor tells you this is too complicated. Why don't you pay, right from the start, 12 insurance dollars? This is what you are going to be charged to age 100. The premium will never change. Isn't this much simpler? The advisor does not tell you that he will be commissioned on 12 insurance dollars instead of 1 insurance dollar. This is not important to know…

With this type of product, the premium will remain the same. The premium is level. However the cost of insurance has not changed. In the first year, the cost of insurance is still 1 insurance dollar and it is paid from your premium of 12 insurance dollars. The 11 insurance dollars remaining is set aside and will go into a reserve. This is the first misrepresentation. Insurers call this a reserve because it gives you the impression it is their money. It is not their money. This is mortality you have prepaid by accepting to pay a level premium. It is your money!

In year 2, you will pay 12 insurance dollars again which will be used to pay 2 insurance dollars of mortality cost. The 10 insurance dollars remaining will go towards the so called reserve. Every year this reserve will increase until the mortality is higher than 12 insurance dollars. In year 13, the mortality cost is 13 insurance dollars. You will still pay 12 insurance dollars but 1 insurance dollar will come out of the reserve to cover the cost of insurance.

What do you think will happen if you surrender this policy in year 13? The insurer and the advisor will tell you nothing of this reserve hoping that you have forgotten about what you have prepaid and this is working… People cancel these policies leaving behind all of the money they have prepaid. The insurer ends up not having to pay a death benefit and gets to cash in on all of your money hidden in the reserve.

Now let's assume there are smart people who know this. Let's assume they see this as an opportunity for them and for you. They make you an offer of buying your policy for 50 cents of the dollar value of the reserve? If the value of the premiums you have prepaid is now worth $50,000 on a policy with $100,000 death benefit, they will give you $25,000 for it. The third party will now own the policy and continue paying the premium. Instead of getting nothing from the insurance company you get a windfall of $25,000 from the third party.

For the third party, this is a good investment because they are buying a policy where they will be paying a premium which will be lower than the mortality cost. For example, they will be paying 12 insurance dollars even if the cost of insurance for you is now 13 insurance dollars. At your death, their investment is realized when they receive the death benefit.

Isn't this better than getting NOTHING for your insurance policy? I think the answer is obvious. Who do you think is not happy? The answer is quite obvious and it is the insurer since they do not get to keep your money. They will still make a profit but that is not what they want. They want to make an insane amount of profit by robbing you.

What insurers are doing to protect their illicit profits is pretty sneaky. They can't prevent you and me from selling our policy. Life insurance is a property and we have the right to enjoy the property we own. It is very difficult to restrict this right. However commercial activities can be easily restricted and the government can prevent someone from organizing a commercial activity built around buying life insurance policies. This is what the insurers did. The insurers paid off a few politicians and it is therefore illegal to buy an insurance policy on a commercial basis in many provinces. The politicians who accepted money from the insurers, through well paid lobbyists, despite all of the independent studies concluding that the buying and selling of insurance should be legal, created a law against the solicitation to buy life policies.

There are no doubts that if financial advisors stood up for the rights of their clients, prohibition of life settlements would have been long gone. Instead advisors have chosen to toe the line and do the insurers' bidding. This will come back to haunt them. Prohibition against life settlements is wrong! Canadians need the income more than the insurers need the extra profit.

The financial industry prefers that a consumer lapse or cancel a life insurance policy rather than receiving an income from this policy.

If a consumer has a T100 with a death benefit of $100,000, the industry wants the consumer to lapse this policy and get nothing in return. If the T100 policy has a Fair Market Value of $50,000, the consumer could instead keep the policy in force and receive an income based on this $50,000 under the forms of a loan. Basically it is a reverse mortgage but the property is life insurance instead of a home.

This is prohibited in most provinces under the guise it is speculation on insurance. How can this be when you still own the policy? When you die the loan is repaid and your beneficiaries receive the rest. There is no speculation here... Politicians will say anything when doing the bidding of the insurers.

The industry also hides the fact that the value of the $50,000 is based largely on the fact that the consumer has prepaid his premiums. As much as 50% of the Fair Market Value can be attributed to this prepayment. The rest is attributed to interest rate and mortality differential. This prepayment belongs to the consumer. It is his money and he should have the right to use this prepayment as a form of income.

It's pretty basic really. If the consumer cancels his policy, the insurer makes $50,000 and never has to pay the death benefit of $100,000. If a viatical settlement is made, the insurer loses $50,000 and will have to pay the death benefit of $100,000. On just one life policy this is a $150,000 difference in the result between the insurers being able to make viaticals illegal and viaticals being legal. Now multiply that $150,000 difference by thousands of policies. Now do you get it Mike?

Again this is not disclosed. Mark my word. There will be a day of reckoning in the future and what goes around will come around. The industry will be held accountable for this considering they are stealing money from the property owned by seniors, people with terminal illness... Here is an example:

Life settlement: Industrial Alliance - Where insanity and

stupidity comes together…

How stupid, ignorant, unintelligent – a one of kind bully – for Industrial Alliance to have made these statements in regards to viatical settlements recently published in the Insurance Journal.

http://journal-assurance.ca/article/assurance-viatique-ia-met-en-garde-ses-conseillers/

First let's be clear. Contrary to what is stated a "viatical settlement" is not a life settlement. It is one kind of life settlement. That differentiation is important to avoid the release of stupid statements. What is a viatical settlement? Here is the definition: an arrangement whereby a person with a terminal illness sells their life insurance policy to a third party for less than its mature value, in order to benefit from the proceeds while alive.

NOW I "WANTS" TO KNOW!!!

Who is in the business to submit application on terminally ill people and which insurer is in the business of issuing policies on terminally ill people? I "WANTS" TO KNOW because I have tons of terminally ill people who want insurance coverage.

Unless the business of insurance has changed since my golden days, insurance is issued when an insurable interest exists. This excludes terminally ill people. So therefore, logic dictates, a logic which seems to be above the brain capacity of anyone at Industrial Alliance, that to take advantage of a viatical settlement, you first have to be insurable; healthy enough to get the insurance.

So this means when you buy insurance, it is not because you are near death, but because you are afraid of what will happen financially at your death and because you care about those you love. Ten, fifteen, twenty… years down the road you are diagnosed with a terminal illness and you are told you have less than 2 years to live. Guess what? You never bought this policy having in mind to do a viatical settlement but shit does happen! That's life.

Now let's see what happens when this happens in real life. Hugh is terminally ill and his doctor gave him 2 years. He applied for a living benefit on his $375,000 Sun Life insurance policy. It was denied. To get hi benefit we had to *threaten CHLIA to put Hugh on TV to resolve this. Then the $100,000 magically appeared. How many times this is happening where they don't have any help, such as the help provided, having no other choice but to cancel their policies? How many?*

The $100,000 was sent by Fedex with not even a cover letter. Sunlife, is this how you deal with terminally ill people? Where is the compassion? At least act professionally because it reflects on us all. And where was the advisor in all of this? Hiding in the hills, fearful that his agent contract would be terminated if he got involved? Is this what this industry has come to? Where was Advocis and where was Chambre Financiere who can't stop saying that consumer protection is their top priority?

I hear it all the times that consumers need advisors. We can't survive without them. To these advisors, here is what I have to say:

A little less acting with the mouth,
A little less acting with the feet,
A little more acting with the heart.

It even rhymes so that you can easily remember what's important.

Now coming back to Industrial Alliance. You are stating that you will cancel the existing policy of a terminally ill policy owner if he enters into a viatical settlement...

How dare you say such a thing? You publicly admit that you will breach a legal contract. How dare you?

You state you are going to sue if a terminally ill client enters into such an arrangement. Money is power... Is this what you are all about?

How dare you say such a thing? This is the definition of legal insanity.

You state that you don't care whether this is legal in any of the provinces. Does this mean Industrial Alliance has become too big to respect provincial laws? Maybe this is the argument I should used to argue that it is time that the business of insurance be legislated and regulated under federal law. I believe you are not yet too big to not respect federal laws.

How dare you say such a thing? Someone at LA is clearly not thinking these thoughts; this person is literally speaking "farting" these thoughts.

So here some news for you and the industry. In September, I am deposing a legal procedure in the Court of Quebec against Manulife in regards to this insanity. You just been added to my list of subpoenas (LA and Sun Life). And when you get to Court, I guarantee you there will be a lot of sick people in the crowd who have been denied their benefits (if they are still alive). Let's see if you have the courage to make the same stupid statements when you are face to face with this crowd and a judge.

And where is the regulator? Where is the Autorite Marche Financier (AMF) because what LA's statements violate several provisions of the Insurance Act and the Act pertaining to the distribution and sale of insurance? LA admitted publicly they were going to break the law and commit fraud against the elderly and sick people!!!

Isn't it their role to ensure the laws of the province of Quebec are respected?

When I ask this question in Court, am I going to find that the "good" people of the AMF were too busy sipping champagne and eating caviar with their "friendly" insurance executives to act and do their job?

A lot of people will condemn the language contained therein. I should be more diplomatic they will say; it is so much more constructive. Bullshit I say! If diplomacy worked, Ontario would not have acted against its own studies to cozy up to the insurance lobbying interests when prohibiting a secondary market for life insurance.

The day I don't use this language and stop calling a dog for what it is; the day I don't get angry when confronted by the pure exploitation of the elderly and people who are sick; it is the day I become a politician and run for election.

May this day never come!

As you can see Mike, I do not have many investment opportunities to create income out of my RRIF. Saving into a RRSP was easy. There were a lot of investment opportunities to create wealth. When you transition to income, it is an entirely different ball game. You can continue investing in the market but then you will be faced with a monster. This monster would like nothing more than to destroy your retirement. This monster is called volatility.

Let's assume your standard financial plan says you'll have enough money to last 25 years. This plan looks so pretty but it is based on nothing real. It is based on a constant rate of return. This type of return does not exist when you invest in an equity investment. Then you retire at the beginning of a typical bear market and you find that your portfolio will last only for 18 years even if you achieve the rate of return that was projected.

Why does this happen?

Let's first look at dollar cost averaging. Dollar cost averaging is traditionally a way to add money to an investment by depositing a set dollar amount on a periodic basis. Let's say you hold an investment during a bull market. Your deposits are buying less and less shares. This will increase the impact on the value of your investment if the market was to drop. Right there you see that dollar cost averaging can't work. Remember when I was saying that people lose their money during transition; well this is a transition.

Dollar cost averaging is a lazy and stupid way to invest. Dollar cost averaging is an efficient way to save but it is an inefficient way to accumulate wealth by achieving a good rate of return.

Dollar cost averaging makes things very simple and very profitable to the financial industry. No matter what happens, they know how much money will get invested in their investment. They get the same amount whether or not the market is up or down. It is very profitable for them. The number of transactions is minimized which is also very profitable to them. Here is a fact for you Mike. Those who bought Canadian equity when it was at its highest at 15,000, when everybody knew it, are not going to recover financially from this. Their retirement is gone. The deposits they made 10 years ago are still worth less than their original value. Maybe in another 10 years the market will be back to 15,000. What a waste of money.

Portfolio failure, meaning you will run out of money during your retirement, is directly related to volatility. This is linked to what is called reverse dollar cost averaging. Instead of making regular deposits, you are making regular withdrawals and again volatility will work against you.

As volatility goes up, you can expect the expected failure rate of a portfolio, when regular withdrawals are made, to rise exponentially. Most retirees don't know this. They are shown instead a nice printout where the rate of return is constant by their advisor. How can they appreciate the link between portfolio volatility and running out of money before age 100?

Converting a constant rate of return into an average rate of return (based on year to year volatile rate of return) is a difficult task to do. Lately, I saw a retirement plan based on 8%. Right there, it's clear that the advisor forgot to mention the MER and his commission. When you add this to the 8% return, you need an 11% gross rate of return to get there. Here is how we can illustrate volatility versus a constant rate of return. If the maximum rate of return you can expect to achieve in any one year is 20%, this mean there is only a difference of 9% between the 20% rate of return and 11% average rate of return. If the maximum you can lose in any one year is -20%, then the difference between -20% and the 11% rate of return is 31%.

Mathematically this means that if in one year, you lose 20%, you will have to earn +20% for about 3 years to make up your loss. For every bad year, you will need 3 good years to achieve this 8% average rate of return equivalent to an 8% constant rate of return. This is impossible. Statistically, this changes volatility and the pattern of returns that is required. You will find that no investments exist which can deliver these results. This phenomenon is called investment divergence.

How can I explain this in a simple manner? When a constant rate of return is used in a retirement plan, advisors are assuming that the constant rate of return can be converted into an average rate of return. It is like assuming that 1 US dollar is the equivalent of 1

Canadian dollar. What do you think will happen when you do the conversion? Advisors are showing retirement plans that are worthless because volatility is excluded.

Even if you were able to stomach the ups and downs of the market, volatility will still get you. The steady timing of withdrawals and the unpredictable swings in the fund's investment value will work against you. When volatility increases, it increases the chances that you'll be taking money out when the portfolio is down, increasing the probability of locking in your losses.

The impact of volatility can be devastating if the negative returns occur early in the withdrawal period. This is where the power of compounded returns will work against you. You will be faced with compounded losses.

To summarize, when volatility is included; if you achieved an 8% average rate of return and you compare the current value of your investment with the value of the investment shown on your retirement plan which is based on a constant rate of return of 8%, you may find that the current value of your investment is lower by as much as 50%. This is how much volatility can impact retirement.

Unless you have a lot of money at retirement, you cannot survive volatility. But then where are you supposed to invest your money?

Just talking about volatility discourages me from ever believing that I could retire one day. Sadly this is not the only problem. There is a major problem with the way the government forces you to take withdrawals out of your RRIF. The government forces you to lock in the losses created by volatility. The government seems to be our biggest enemy when you try to save for retirement.

It is interesting to note that absolutely nobody in the financial industry talks about the most important flaw with a RRIF. I believe this is because it would result in the loss of a lot of management and commission fees. Let's assume you have $100,000 in GICs and $100,000 into an equity mutual fund. The market crashes by 50% and your fund is now worth $50,000. Your RRIF minimum is 10%.

Your first problem is that the RRIF minimum withdrawal is based on last end of year value. So you will be required to take 10% of $200,000 and not 10% of $150,000. Now it would make sense to take the whole $20,000 out of your GICs to avoid realizing your loss on the equity side. YOU CANNOT DO THIS!!! Why? The reason is simple; each investment is considered an individual RRIF and you must take your minimum withdrawal individually from each individual RRIF.

Why is the government telling your where to withdraw your money? Is this right? If you do a research on this you will see how this problem is well hidden.

By having RRIF minimums applied in such fashion, it discourages people in keeping liquidities to fund their short term retirement income. This keep people invested more than they should be and allows the industry to earn greater fees and commissions.

I knew a financial planner who used to recommend to his clients that they keep 5 years of future income into a low risk and liquid investment. How did he do this? He used a segregated fund which unlike a mutual fund is a policy contract. The RRIF minimum therefore applies to the segregated fund contract and not to the individual seg fund investments offered in the contract.

He used a segregated fund named Maritime Life Investment Account which was offering GICs and various equity funds in the same segregated fund contract. He would keep 5 years of income into the GICs which allowed the client to take more risk on the equity side. If the market crashed by 50%, he could take the whole RRIF minimum from the GICs. When the market was high he would realized the gain by taking the entire RRIF minimum from equity. This is what he called managing a transition effectively. Most advisors don't do this at all and clients are losing a lot of money.

When Manulife bought Maritime Life, this product was discontinued. Ask yourself why? I had a customer who worked at Manulife and one day we were discussing this. He told me how high level executives would become upset when there was too much money in GICs. The wholesaler would then be dispatched and unleashed on the advisor to convince them to fully invest their clients in the market. This is why! It is all about profits...They don't care about us.

This is why you will find it extremely difficult to find such wrapped investment. It is amazing for an industry to state to consumers not to change their RRSP investments when the market is down to avoid realizing losses and then have this industry being oblivious to the same problem when RRIF are involved...

Tip fifteen: Understand that RRIF as a retirement solution is a fairy tale story where you don't get to live happily thereafter. However if you don't have a pension plan, it's the only solution available. As a result you have to understand and manage the pitfalls surrounding this product. You cannot count on a financial advisor to do this. Financial advisors are only interested in showing you a rosy picture so they can make a quick sale.

11 RETIREMENT AND PENSION PLANS

> *The roots of the looming retirement crisis were created when the financial industry was able to convince the government that private savings was the way to fund retirement. It is interesting to note that those in government who voted in favor of this strategy did not decide to participate in it; keeping instead their very rich pension plan… (The Poor Bartender)*

Mike, do you wish you had a pension plan? Like me you've been excluded from having access to the most efficient way of providing for retirement just because you happen to live and work in a rural area. Without big employers who can fund generous pensions, we are denied access to this form of pension. However we pay income taxes which are used to provide big money to big corporations. Why should you and I pay taxes to subsidize the big pension plans of these big companies when we don't have any?

Why am I paying higher business taxes and municipal taxes to pay for the pension of municipal employees? They should also be paying higher taxes to subsidize my retirement. Life isn't fair…

A Pollara Survey in 2006 found that "Responding to the question why did you invest in a mutual fund? 85% replied they were persuaded to do so by someone who provided me with advice and guidance…"

Now this important and I mentioned this before. It explains why people invest in mutual funds despite the fact that Canadian pension fund participants achieve much higher returns. This is proven. In fact a paper was written in 2007 about this and it was called the $25 billion haircut. This paper showed that Canadians were losing about $25 billion every year in fees and lower returns. If we compound this loss for the last 10 years we are talking about trillions of dollars. This becomes the size of the mortgage bubble in the USA which almost destroyed the world economy. We could call this the retirement bubble.

Why is this happening? The answer is simple. The industry has convinced us that we are too stupid to understand finance and investments. So we need them and their advice. Their advice is simple. Buy mutual funds… You know what is the difference between a mutual fund and a pension plan? Mutual funds are managed to generate profits. Pension plans are managed to achieve the highest return for its participants. It is insanity for our government to worry about ABM fees when this is happening. The $25 billion haircut is a paper to read.

Anyway, this is why we need a very stiff drink that will put some hair on your chest to discuss this topic. I highly recommend a Godfather. Created during the 70's in the USA, the origin of the Godfather is uncertain. Some say it was the favored cocktail of Marlon Brando. It's made with 1 1/2 oz of Scotch (or Bourbon) and ¾ oz of Amaretto Almond Liqueur.

Just pour both the Scotch and Amaretto over ice into an old fashioned glass. You stir slightly like this. Then take a sip and reflect on the Godfather movie. This drink is not for amateurs but the same would apply to pensions. However advisors, who are truly the amateurs when it comes down to their knowledge of pension, keep providing advice on this subject. It is therefore not surprising that their advice is in line with their wallets.

I have observed the demise of the Defined Benefit pension plan because it was too costly. These are plans where the benefit is defined so you will know exactly what you're going to get at retirement. Most of these plans were in a shortfall position and the employers responsible to fund these plans decided to quit on their responsibilities. Instead of addressing the issue, the government allowed retirement to become the sole responsibility of the employee through the use of Defined Contributions plan and RRSPs.

A Defined Contribution plan is a plan where you know what you will contribute but you don't know the level of retirement income your contributions will generate. It will all depend on how you invest these contributions. So you are now assuming the risk associated with your retirement. It is a big risk. Chances are that members of that pension plan will also be faced with a shortfall at retirement. However this shortfall won't be as large as if the member had invested in a RRSP since the MER of this type pension is only in average .75%.

It seems weird to me that we expect employees to achieve better results when using RRSPS that have a Management Expense Ratio 300% to 400% higher than what apply to Defined Contribution pension plans. Before, employees could expect 5% to 10% of their retirement assets going towards fees and MERs. Now about 40% of the retirement assets of employees are going towards fees if you're using an RRSP.

We then wonder why Canadians do not have enough money to retire. We wonder why a retirement crisis is looming over us…

Can I tell you a story? It's a true one, and – unfortunately – I have seen it happened more than once. Here it goes:

Jack, a friend of mine, was leaving his job, and this meant he was going to lose access to his Defined Benefit plan. He got a small sheet of paper from his company, asking him to choose between getting a lifetime monthly pension at retirement, or taking a lump sum now, transferable (at least in part) to a locked in retirement savings plan.

Over the next few weeks, Jack wavered between these two choices. The monthly income amount seemed small compared to the commutation value. He also did not have a lot of faith in the management of his company to take care of him for the rest of his life. On the other hand, he had never paid much attention to investing before, and could not imagine how he would invest that much money.

Sixty days is a small amount of time to make that kind of decision. The deadline was looming and Jack finally decided he needed some help. He made his mind to call the investment advisor his brother-in-law was using assuming he would be dealing with a professional who would be able to explain the pros and cons of both options allowing Jack to weigh these options rationally against each other. The advisor even came to Jack's house to help him.

The advisor told Jack to take the lump sum without doing much research. This was the best choice and the advisor would be happy to invest that money for him. He had charts that showed the growth of an investment over the amount of time Jack had left until he retired. The charts looked so good. It was amazing the amount of money he would be able to withdraw every year at retirement. "Don't worry about risk," the advisor said "you are going to have access to the best mutual funds with a four or five star rating. Their great fund managers will look after your money."

Jack was impressed. Seeing how the lump sum offer grew over time made the lifetime pension seemed even smaller by comparison. Being in control of his own retirement money; when he had the help of an advisor sounded better than leaving his money in the hands of his old company run by managers he did not trust. Jack decided to take the commutation value.

This so called advisor had been very quick in advising my friend in taking the commutation value talking about the merits of investing the money under his management and the management of mutual funds managers.

I asked Jack this simple question: "What is your crossover point for your rate of return?"

"I don't know," he answered.

"Well you should know because this should have been a big subject of discussion between you and the advisor."

"He never mentioned this."

"Well let me explained what the crossover rate of return is. When your employer calculated the commutation value of your pension plan, he had to make an assumption as to a future rate of return. He then used that rate to determine the commutation value of your pension plan. So far you are following me, right?"

He nodded his head with understanding.

"Let's assume your employer used a 5% rate of return. For you to take the commutation value of the pension plan solely based on FUTURE RETURNS as proposed by this advisor, you would have to be able to earn more than 5%. How would you do this? No GICs provide this type of return. No bond investments either. This leaves the market and mutual funds. However as soon as you invest in mutual funds, Management Expense Ratios are deducted from what you will earn. Let's assume the MER is 3%. The advisor and the mutual fund would have to provide you a gross return of 8% for you to break even on the switch. Is this clear?"

"Yes."

"Good. But I am not finished. The 5% used in the calculation of the commutation value can be viewed as a guaranteed rate of return; a risk free return. The 8% is not guaranteed and you will have to take risk to get this return. This means for taking this risk you need to be rewarded by getting what we could call a risk premium. I don't know about you but for me to take this kind of risk I would need to get a significant reward and I would ask 2%. This means that the advisor and fund manager would have to show me that they can generate a 10% rate of return. This is the minimum to do the switch. What is the likelihood of this?"

"So you mean I should not take the commutation value..."

"No I did not say this. I'm not offering you financial advice because I don't know your situation and while I have more knowledge than most of these people who call themselves "financial advisor" I don't believe I have the knowledge to provide you advice on this decision. This is a very complex decision. My goal here was to show you that the advisor you were dealing with was misrepresenting his knowledge and abilities. On top of that, this advisor was in a conflict of interest. Did he discuss this?

"No."

"Well he should have. He should have told you that for this transaction he was in fact acting solely as a commissioned representative who could not provide advice on the pension plan. As such, if you kept the pension plan he would not get a cent of commission while he could potentially get hundreds of thousands of dollars in commission if you took the commutation value and invested it with him. This should have been disclosed to you and he should have requested that you sign a waiver on this conflict of interest.'

"Hundreds of thousands of dollars in commission; is this possible?"

"Yes. This represents the present value of the total amount of commission that he will receive. Studies have shown that regular MERs will reduce you asset by as much as 40%."

"So who can help me?"

"You have 2 choices. Find a financial advisor who does have the knowledge to provide advice on this type of decision. There are some but they represent 1% of the total sales force. You would have to accept the existence of a conflict of interest. You second choice is to hire an actuary who will provide you with a valuation of your choices. This will cost you money but when you put this cost in perspective; when you consider the amount of MER you will have to pay if you take the commutation value; it is worth it. When you have the independent review of the actuary in hand, then you are informed and ready to deal with a financial sales representative if your report seems to indicate you should take the commutation value."

Mike, it's interesting to note that Jack never consulted an actuary. He did not want to pay one thousand or two thousand dollars for an actuary. People are funny like this. They would rather lose hundreds of thousands of dollars instead of paying one or two thousand dollars.

We have to ask ourselves why has the government not impose a limit of the fees applied to RRSPs when the same government let employers off their responsibility in providing a pension program to their employees?

Mike I have proven to you that just a 2% management fee will reduce the assets of a RRSP by as much as 40% over a period of 35 years. Legislating a top fee of .5% would increase retirement benefits provided by RRSPs and RRIFs by more than 30%. This would have a tremendous impact on the retirement crisis. Instead the government blames us for this crisis telling us we did not save enough. I think you see the irony…

It is clear the financial industry would be against this. They would state that such a fee would prevent access to advice. So what! The Canadians who have a Defined Contribution plan are doing very well without such advice. Why do you necessarily need an advisor? If you feel you need an advisor, then it's up to you to pay a fee to this advisor such as 1%. Even by paying that 1%you would still be paying a lower MER than what is currently charged for most mutual funds.

When you think about it Mike, why has the government chosen not to improve the Canada Pension Plan instead of introducing the RRSP? I would have agreed in paying more money into the Canada Pension Plan instead of contributing to an RRSP. This would have been great. But I supposed someone had to pay to employ all of these advisors who would not be able to do anything else…

Let's come back to the original subject. What should have Jack done? Nothing could match his defined pension plan. However he was scared. He was scared that his employer was making promises he could not keep. He was scared that the company would go bankrupt living the pension plan underfunded. This should not happen. The government should require a yearly audit and make it illegal for employers to run a deficit in a pension plan. But again the government is not doing its job and it is the people who are paying for this.

Do you know Mike how many people have sat where you are telling me how they lost it all? There was Betty whose employer decided to move from a defined benefit to a defined contribution plan. She had a great plan with indexing. The employer cancelled the indexing which would have allowed her to keep up with the cost of living. The employer had not funded the defined benefit plan properly and basically decided to cut retiree benefits by 33%.

Is this right?

I met some of the employees of Burns Meats which was sold to Maple Leaf. It was found that bad and illegal investments were made with the money of the pension plan. Some employees saw their monthly benefit of $500 go to $300. Already $500 is a pittance. Imagine you're left with $300.

Is this right?

Then there is Coldstream that went bankrupt. During the time Coldstream was in operations, the employee often took no wage increases for better benefits under their pension plan. Coldstream filed for bankruptcy and moved its operations to a sister operation. You see the scam. It is perfectly legal however. The pension plan had a solvency deficiency ratio of 70% and under the law in Manitoba pension benefits were reduced accordingly. So people who did the right thing by not taking wage increases had to accept a loss of benefit of about 70%.

Is this right? While this is happening, politicians who are supposed to protect these employees will enjoy a nice pension plan funded by our taxes.

THE POOR BARTENDER

The example of Nackawick not far from where we are is the perfect example of this. The Nackawic pulp mill was owned Parsons & Whittemore (PW) which was a private American company owned by the Landegger family. Since it was a private company that doesn't trade on the stock exchange most of its financial data was hidden and is still hidden. However it is easy to know that PW is one of the largest pulp companies in the world with more $1 billion in annual revenue. PW also made hundreds of millions of dollars of profits at Nackawic. However PW was legally allowed to declare bankruptcy. Isn't this crazy? The employee lost in the bankruptcy more than 31 million dollars in compensation and had to accept a 30% decrease in pension benefits.

I could continue telling you stories but what is the point.

Do you get rid of a pension plan by transferring it to a private retirement plan or do you keep it? I can't give you an answer Mike. Sometimes the answer will be obvious. If the break even rate is low such as 2%, then I would assume you have enough knowledge to beat the pension plan and you should take the cash. If your company is currently in a deficit position, they are required to let you know. Depending on the reasons, it may be a wise move to take the commutation value. But these are the exceptions. In most cases, the choice won't be that obvious. This is why you should get help but the only help that matters is objective help, without conflicts of interest.

It is not an easy thing to determine the true nature of the commutation value provided to you for the purpose of convincing you to drop out of a Defined Benefit pension plan. Normally, both the plan and the former employee should be indifferent about whether the commutation value or deferred pension is taken. But this is not the case when you include the value of ancillary benefits.

Remember that Jack was 50. He could take a pension of $1,000 at age 65. He could also elect to take the pension as early as age 55 but the pension amount would be reduced if he elected this option. The commutation value of the pension was about $70,000.

To have an income to age 100, he would have to earn 5.1%. In 15 years or age 65, when he is ready to retire the commutation value would be worth around $148,000. This amount should provide him with an income of $1,000 to age 100 at that return but it is not. Why? Because there is also a mortality component hidden in the assumption. The company will assume that if you had kept the pension plan, you would have probably died before age 100. This is reflected in the commutation value. As a result, at 5.1%, the commutation value would only provide $1,000 income to Jack to age 86. Jack would have to earn more than 7% to get an income to age 100. When you add the MER to this 7%, it becomes impossible to beat the pension plan.

WHEN TAKING THE COMMUTATION VALUE YOU ARE TAKING BACK THE RISK OF LIVING LONGER...

Many people decide to transfer their commutation value because they believe their families will get nothing from the plans if they were to die. They are wrong. If they die before they retire, the plan must pay the spouse or beneficiary at least the commutation value of the pension. At retirement, the employee has the option to elect a pension that continues to the spouse like 60% of the pension amount.

And Mike, remember what I told you about volatility. To match the pension guaranteed amount, Jack will have to take a lot of risk to age 100 when truly we should take less and less risk as we get older.

If you have a Defined Benefit pension plan, you are one of the lucky minorities who will receive a guaranteed pension amount for life. This is worth a lot of money. However you are at the mercy of your employer.

If you have a Defined Contribution plan, you lose this guarantee of a life income. However, you are still in a better position since most employers will match your contributions and the fees associated with the pension plan are very low; around .75%. You have to maximize what you are putting in knowing that it won't be enough. As I said, if most employers can't provide a pension plan to age 100 without going broke, how can you do it?

If you don't have access to a pension plan and you rely on RRSP, you are one of the unlucky one. You are faced with high fees, poor advice full of conflict of interest and a badly designed investment vehicle.

Tip sixteen: "When it comes down to deciding what to do with a pension plan, it is worth it to spend a few thousand dollars to save a few hundred thousands of dollars."

# 12 LIFE INSURANCE

> *There are so many ways of losing money when buying insurance because consumers don't understand what it is and because they do not like the subject matter, they won't ask any questions. It is therefore not surprising that the life insurance industry evolved into a predatory system; preying on the ignorance of consumers while being fueled by rich commissions paid upfront to ensure that consumers don't get any service, guaranteeing they will remain ignorant…(The Poor Bartender)*

Mike I could write a book solely on how not to lose money when buying life insurance. The life insurance industry has been built on misrepresentations and outright lies. Its culture is corrupted. The life insurance industry is a master at blaming others for its excesses while making enormous profits.

Just take the vanishing premium fraud. Not one insurer has admitted its guilt. They all blamed the so called advisors…

Contrary to what we believe, the Canadian judges have allowed the insurers to pay damages equivalent to a dime for every dollar of profit they made. The Class Actions that took place in Canada were a failure compared to the Class Actions in the US. This is an indictment of our justice system which favors big corporations. Sometimes the truth comes out. In this case, it came out in a personal lawsuit against Manulife. I think I have a paper on this. Feel free to read it while I am preparing you a special drink. It's not an old drink. In fact it's fairly new. It was created to illustrate deception. It is called An Empty Cocktail for Mitch McConnell.

Senator Mitch McConnell was a senate minority leader in the U.S.A. He was involved in a tough reelection fight with Alison Lundergan Grimes, the secretary of state in Kentucky. McConnell used deception to hide the consequences of repealing Obamacare.

This cocktail was designed to show McConnell's deceit with a twist that really brings it together. This cocktail uses 2.5 oz bourbon whiskey, 1 oz sweet vermouth, 2 to 3 dashes aromatic bitters, 1 brandied cherry for garnish and 4 ice cubes. You fill a martini glass with ice to chill it. Add the whiskey, sweet vermouth and bitters into a shaker with ice and mix. Pour the mixture into martini glass. Here is the twist; before handing the drink to a friend, distract them with a magic trick while dumping the drink contents into the trash. Hand the empty martini glass to your friend and drink as many as you like. You'll never get drunk.

It is a perfect drink to illustrate all of the deceit surrounding insurance except I won't be pouring it down the trash. So Mike you can read this while I am taking orders from my other customers.

Ward against Manulife:

[4] It is my opinion that the Plaintiffs/Defendants by Counterclaim can fairly be described as "scapegoats". In other words, the Defendant seeks to persuade this Court to blame the Plaintiffs/Defendants by Counterclaim for the conduct of others and, in particular, for its own failings.

In Insurance Ward against Manulife, Insurance Ward was asking damages in the amount of about $1 million and punitive damages in the amount of $500,000. As stated by the judge, here is a summary of the claims made by Insurance Ward:

[5] The Plaintiff, Reginald Ward Senior ... (now 71) is a licensed life insurance agent and is president of Reg Ward Insurance... Reg Ward has been a licensed insurance agent since 1967 and later obtained his chartered life underwriter designation (CLU). His business was concerned with the sale of life insurance, RRSP's and related products...Reg Ward is the father of his co-defendant by counterclaim, Steve Ward. Steve Ward, at all relevant times, was an insurance

agent.

[11] Monarch's assets and liabilities were purchased by North American Life Assurance Company (NAL) in 1983. On January 1, 1996, NAL merged with Manulife. In his early years with Monarch, Mr. Ward was provided with written information concerning various Monarch products. This included information concerning dividends payable to insureds, cash surrender value projections, and rates. All applications for insurance were required to be submitted for approval by Mr. Ward to the Oshawa office. The Oshawa regional office, under the branch manager's direction, would then check and complete the application forms following which they would be sent to Monarch's head office for final approval and policy issuance. This type of process, basically, was followed by the subsequent insurers with whom Mr. Ward was associated – i.e., NAL and Manulife.

As the years passed, the insurance products available through Monarch became more sophisticated. Throughout his entire relationship with Monarch, and indeed, with NAL and Manulife, Mr. Ward and other agents or representatives were always under pressure to sell products that would result in the insured, or other product owner, leaving his/her money with the insurer. For instance, insureds were urged to allow policy dividends to accumulate and be used to purchase additional benefits or, where appropriate, to be used to reduce the costs of future premiums.

This reveals the existence of a culture of deceit existing at the insurance level. The judge is starting to refer to the vanishing premium scandal from a public perspective and fraud from a consumer perspective. Insurers were held partly accountable monetarily for their actions through class actions but this did not result in a change of culture. Those who pressured advisors and those who knowingly provided the wrong information to advisors were not held accountable for their actions.

[22] In on or about 1982-1983, "premium offset" (or vanishing premium) policies came into use. These policies became attractive to purchasers of life insurance and, in various forms, became the product of choice well into the 1990's. Agents were encouraged to sell the premium offset products. Owners/insureds were attracted to the premium offset formula because the result was that they would not have to pay insurance premiums forever.
[23] Agents, initially, were provided with "illustrations" prepared at Monarch's

head office. Later, these illustrations emanated from the branch offices of NAL and Manulife. The illustrations were to be used as a selling tool – to demonstrate to the potential client that he/she could purchase long-term life insurance coverage, but be required to pay premiums only during a restricted period. The agents were required to add some personal information and other details to the illustrations. Completed versions were then delivered to the client by the Wards.

[25] Initially, as a result of information received from the insurance companies, agents such as Mr. Ward advised clients that they would probably have to pay premiums for more than 8 or 9 years before obtaining a premium holiday. This estimate of time, of course, was based, to a large extent, on expectations regarding how the general economy would perform. When the economy did improve, the estimate of time was reduced to 8 or 9 years. Later, this time projection was increased to 12 or 14 years because of economic conditions.

[26] I find that Reg and Steve Ward appreciated the fact that these estimates were not guaranteed because anticipated dividends could not be forecast with absolute certainty. However, I find that the Wards, and other agents, were the recipients of representations from the insurance companies, which they believed, that there would be no difficulty for insurance companies to meet these non-guaranteed projections notwithstanding that some of the relevant written information that prospective purchasers would be given contained written qualifications. A very positive environment existed – an environment created by the insurance companies which were passed on to insurance purchasers through the agents.

[27] The agents were provided with computer-generated documentation that appeared to confirm the reasons for the optimism. These projections were quite sophisticated and were the result of work by actuaries and other professionals at head office. The Wards, like other agents, were not the authors of this optimism nor were they advised about the details leading to the justification for it.

[28] Exhibit 2(a), tab 27, is a document from Manulife's productions. There is some dispute in the evidence whether this is a Manulife document. However, the evidence is that it came from Manulife's productions. I find that it is an example of a sales tool used by insurers in the 1980's. The document is entitled *"SALES TRACK EXPLAINING PREMIUM OFFSET ILLUSTRATION"*.

[66] However, in the spring of 1995, NAL discovered that Steve Ward had been involved in a number of questionable selling and servicing issues with clients dating back at least three years. The malfeasance included, among other things, forged signatures and the payment of premiums on behalf of clients. As a result of the discovery of these issues, Steve Ward resigned. His resignation was accepted. NAL withdrew its sponsorship of Steve Ward's life insurance license and filed a

Notice of Termination of Agent…
A letter of resignation was received from Steve Ward, effective May 3, 1995 in light of discussions with North American Life concerning his paying premiums for clients and signing documents on their behalf.
[67] On May 15, 1995, NAL sent a memo to "All Members of the Central Ontario Financial Centre", as follows: Steve Ward has elected to leave North American Life in order to pursue other responsibilities within Ward Insurance Services Ltd.
[68] On May 19, 1995, a notice was sent to policyholders for whom Steven Ward was responsible. This memo said, among other things: You are a valued customer and we are pleased to tell you that your account will be serviced by Mr. Reg Ward of Reg Ward Insurance Services Ltd. in Cobourg.
[72] Blair Anderson, Manulife's in-house legal counsel, in early 1997, when dealing with the claims' process arising out of a class action against Manulife, focused his attention on some complaints received from policyholders with respect to the Wards. In an internal memo, dated March 5, 1997, (exhibit 8(a), tab 4), Mr. Anderson said:
I understand you are investigating Reg Ward. I have spoken [sic] to Lynda Campbell in audit and it appears that Steve Ward was selling whole life policies on a POP basis when there was no such option to do that. In addition it appears we have had some knowledge for some time that even though Steve resigned he continues to place business with us through his father. This case appears to have implications for the class action litigation. Gord and I would like to discuss this situation with you and Eric. Are you on calendars? If you are I will get Sheila to set up a meeting to discus
[75] In my opinion, this investigation took on a life of its own. At a very early stage, Reg Ward was unjustly condemned.

The opinion of the judge here is interesting. The reason the investigation took a life of its own is because Manulife took the role of the regulator. This was a conflict of interest. Steve Ward infraction should have been investigated by the regulator and it illustrates the danger of an insurer taking on that role because in the end what will be decided will be based on what is good for the company without any regards as to the safety of the public.

[76] By mid-April, without seeking an explanation from Reg Ward, it was determined that Manulife should file a complaint against both Reg and Steve Ward with the Ontario Insurance Commission…

[80] On May 20, 1997, Manulife executives, Barry Hall and Phil Farley, arrived unannounced at Ward Ltd.'s office in Cobourg. They met alone with Reg Ward and began by questioning him concerning the need for an insurance license. They advised him that Steve Ward was unlicensed. Reg Ward initially replied that this was not so. I find that, at this time, Mr. Ward genuinely believed that Steve Ward was, in fact, licensed. As noted above, Reg Ward was aware that an application had been submitted and his understanding was that there had been some red tape delaying the process, but that Steve Ward was legally permitted to sell policies...

[86] In early July, Manulife contacted the Ontario Insurance Commission by telephone and advised it of its "grave concerns around the selling practices of both Reg and Steve" and that Manulife would be making a report to the Commission so that it "will have the information when she is considering the issuance of a license to Steve." ("She", meaning Joanne Fortin of the Commission)

[87] The complaint that was subsequently sent to the Commission was the result of the input of a number of Manulife officials. At the time it was sent, Manulife was aware that since 1996 it had received only five complaints about the Wards and that four of these were concerning Steve. I find that the evidence that was subsequently produced at trial with respect to this particular complaint against Reg Ward did not reveal any wrongdoing on his part that was deserving of some sort of discipline or sanction.

[88] On July 2, 1997, a decision was taken by Mr. Anderson and others to terminate "Reg Ward's contract with Manulife." In a memo from Jacqueline Mitchell to Mr. Hall on July 3rd she confirmed that decision and then said'...

[89] Mr. Hall responded immediately as follows: My bias is to terminate with normal contractual notice and not mess around with any "breach of contract" argument. We have the ability to alert OIC of the extent of the issues and encourage a "suitability" Hearing. We have a ton of clients to deal with in the Cobourg area, and I see little value in the "cause" position. Just my view.

...

[91] On July 16, 1997, a termination letter was hand delivered to Reg Ward by Mr. Farley and another Manulife employee. The letter is addressed to both Reg Ward and Reg Ward Insurance Services Ltd...

No less than five new agents were assigned to the Ward block of business. Obviously, Manulife wanted to preserve for itself 30 years of Ward efforts.

[96] On July 17, 1997, Steve Ward wrote to Mr. Hall to draw certain facts to his attention. Reg Ward was not aware of the existence of this letter until much later. Among other things, Steve Ward said:

...

First of all I can honestly say that at no time prior to your visit to our office, along with Mr. Farley, did my father have any idea that my license was no longer in force. Indeed neither had I been so informed until I contacted the O.I.C. after your visit. To punish him for something he did not know anything about would be like saying that Mr. Farley and the rest of the management team in Oshawa are also at fault simply because they run the office through which the business in question flowed, and of course, it is obviously not their fault either. At this point in order to understand the chain of events that brought us to this situation I should begin at the beginning...

[103] In August and September 1997, Reg Ward wrote to his clients advising that he was no longer under contract with Manulife, but that he was still in the insurance business. He asked them to sign an "agent of record" letter. This resulted in about a 95% return rate. By this time, many of his clients had already been contacted by other Manulife agents to whom the Wards' clients had been assigned. Manulife objected to Mr. Ward's attempts to remain in business and, on September 17, 1997, wrote to Mr. Ward as follows:

It has come to my attention that you are sending a letter to Manulife policy owners suggesting that you can service their policies if they sign an enclosed letter.

In the last paragraph of my letter sent to you dated July 16, 1997 it clearly states "As of August 15th, 1997 Reg Ward Insurance Services Limited will be removed as servicing agent on all business placed by the producer with Manulife and a new servicing agent will be assigned". In fact a new servicing agent has been assigned to all of the business that you placed with Manulife! This letter that you are sending to Manulife policy owners may confuse these policy owners. We do not want you to service any Manulife policy owners. If you do not stop attempting to service any Manulife policies immediately we will freeze your commission account.

[104] Manulife further responded with a series of letters addressed by it to Mr. Ward's clients. Among other things, the purpose of these letters was to advise the clients of Mr. Ward's status and to introduce the newly assigned servicing agents. Obviously, the Ward clients were in a state of confusion. Many of the clients wrote to Manulife indicating that they wished to keep Reg Ward as their agent. This led to the following series of internal e-mails:

Date: Tuesday, 21 October 1997 11:40 am ET
To: RUTLEDGE.RAYWYN, CORRIGAN.LAURIE, KAUNTZ.SUSAN,
WEHRLE.BRETT
From: FURLANO.JOHN
...

Thought I would sent [sic] an Email out to give some news concerning the Customer Confirmation forms that have been returned. To date, we have 21 cases where the client has advised us in writing that they wish to keep Reg as their agent. This is a pretty high total in relation to the total number of responses that we have received.

I am wondering if we should take the time to develop one standard letter for these clients. Should legal be involved in this at all? Also, are we going to stand firm on not letting Reg service these p/h's, even if there is a chance that we may lose their business?

...

The judge commented here: "The self-serving nature of this and other messages is startling."

[107] Exhibit 8(a), tab 53, is a November 12, 1997 memo from Mr. Anderson to a number of executives, including John Fessenden, a senior Manulife Finance Officer. The memo is an indication of the unwarranted conclusions that were being reached within Manulife with respect to Mr. Ward. The memo reads as follows:

We have had a flurry of activity on Reg's block of business. Susan Kauntz and Barb Hunter will be providing summaries ASAP. 3 issues arise:

1. Reg is clearly trying to disturb [sic] his inforce block

2. We have evidence of sales practices that must be reported to the OIC

3. We have evidence of sales practices that probably should be reported to the police.

Reg is in breach of the terms of Barry's letter of July 25, 1997. There are likely to be chargebacks. We should be immediately suspending his pay and invoke the 36 month hold back provision of his contract. John, can you please advise if you are prepared to do that?

We should be writing to the OIC and pursuing [sic] the OIC vigorously to get his license suspended. We should also [sic] be putting together a package and contacting the police to see if they are prepared to investigate. Jacqueline, I trust you will coordinate this? I will gladly help you with this. Please refer to Barb Hunter and Linda Campbell for details of our concerns. This letter should be going ASAP. Coburg is a small community. Reg has his clients rallying around him at this point. However, I don't think it would take much to expose Reg given what information we already have.

[127] On October 13, 1998, the Ontario Insurance Commission reported to Manulife with respect to Steve Ward. Steve Ward was charged with selling insurance without a license, pleaded guilty, and was fined $500. The Commission and Steve Ward entered into an agreement whereby he would remain out of the

insurance business as far as life, disability; accident and general insurance were concerned for a period of five years. Four years later, on November 8, 2002, the Commission wrote to Reg Ward as follows...
However Manulife totally ignored the decision of the regulator as the employees involved were so bent on destroying Mr. Ward as proved by this heinous message:
[129] On March 17, 1999, Mr. Ward's then solicitor, David Jewitt, wrote to Barry Hall of Manulife objecting to Mr. Fessenden's July 21st letter. Mr. Jewitt's position was that Mr. Ward's persistency had remained at approximately 90%. Legal action was threatened. Mr. Jewitt also took exception with the earlier correspondence to the effect that Mr. Ward was not entitled to renewal commissions on policies issued prior to April 1, 1991. Despite Mr. Jewitt's letter, Manulife did not reverse its position. Manulife advised Mr. Jewitt that, it "had determined that your clients had been engaged in a sustained pattern of misselling." Mr. Jewitt wrote again on November 1, 1999, requesting details regarding the alleged deterioration in persistency.
[130] Mr. Anderson, on behalf of Manulife, replied to Mr. Jewitt under cover of his letter of March 31, 1999, (see Exhibit 8(b), tab 100). The tone of his letter is quite aggressive, especially the following paragraph:

We are also planning, upon receipt of several of the current outstanding settlements, to pursue a meeting with the Commercial Fraud Unit of the RCMP to determine whether or not it would be appropriate to have criminal charges laid against your clients in relation to their activities in the sale of these policies.
[131] One of the agents approached by Manulife to take over part of the Ward business was Alexander Rutherford. Mr. Rutherford, in a letter dated July 13, 1999 to Manulife, summarized the relevant history as follows: (see Exhibit 8(b), tab 104)
...

I was approached by Mark Lomow – Sales Manager of Manulife in September 1997, to do a marketing plan to contact 1500 policy owners. He explained what a great opportunity this would be for me to take over a block of business from another agent, Reg Ward, with whom Manulife no longer had business dealings with as they were investigating into his dealings. Mark made big commitments to assist with the transfer of the business and he said Reg Ward would not be in business much longer. I would be paid a servicing fee of $2000 per month until Reg's license was revoked and then I would receive the renewal commissions.

At this point Manulife lost view of what was right. Someone was standing up to them and they had to be destroyed. As a result, employees of Manulife hatched a scheme to destroy Mr. Ward. To destroy him, Manulife had to generate client complaints against Mr. Ward. Manulife following a class action in regards to vanishing premium was in the process of settling this class action. All of Manulife agents had sold this product under the recommendation of Manulife. As a result, all advisors of Manulife were facing client complaints in regards to the sale of these products. Manulife decided that it would isolate Mr. Ward from other advisors by refusing to settle some of the claims of his clients and by stating that Mr. Ward was personally responsible and liable for the sale of this concept and product.

[232] Manulife argues that written and oral representations made to policyholders by the Wards were wrong, misleading, and were a fundamental misrepresentation regarding the nature of the insurance policies in question. In my opinion, Manulife is, in any event, estopped from seeking contribution from the Wards notwithstanding that it paid substantial monies to members of the class. Manulife was clearly complicit in the overselling techniques that were used to sell policies; was aware, or should have been aware, of what had been transpiring over several years; and, most importantly, encouraged the sales tactics which it presently challenges. Manulife, and it would seem, other insurers, had an early optimistic view of the potential for premium offset policies because of the overly optimistic opinions they obtained from their own experts. The Wards were inspired by this optimism. I have not been persuaded that Manulife has demonstrated any deliberate wrongful or negligent conduct on the part of the Wards; however, as aforesaid, if there is any negligent conduct on their part, Manulife was a major contributor.

[233] Manulife, having encouraged and invited the Wards to aggressively market its products, cannot now look to them to compensate it for the consequences of such conduct. Some of the allegations of wrongdoing pleaded against Manulife in the class action, although not conceded by Manulife in the class action settlement, were apparent in the evidence which I heard during the course of this trial. Manulife cannot now be heard to say that the agents/brokers/representatives should have conducted themselves differently. Even if I am incorrect in my opinion that Manulife is estopped from pursuing its set-off or counterclaim, it is my further opinion that the evidence upon which Manulife relies to prove its claims of misrepresentation falls far short of satisfying the burden on it to prove such wrongdoing on a balance of probabilities. In particular, Manulife's evidence falls far short of supporting its allegation or argument that "Reg Ward and Steve Ward made these representations with wanton disregard for their accuracy and lack of truth."

Interesting stuff right? I think this demonstrate the lack of ethics and honesty existing in the insurance industry.

MORTGAGE INSURANCE:

Now let's talk about insurance. Let's start with the simpler insurance which is mortgage insurance.

Is mortgage insurance bad? First Mike, you have to separate the propaganda from the truth and the insurance industry is good at propaganda.

The insurance industry tries to blame the banks for selling a less than perfect product. But who is responsible for this situation? The bank would love to sell regular life insurance but who is opposed to this; it is the insurance industry. The insurance is blaming the banks for selling a faulty product that the same industry is forcing the banks to sell.

If there is something wrong with a house recently built; do you blame the builder or the seller? You blame the builder. The insurers are the ones who are creating and manufacturing these mortgage insurance products. Therefore they are responsible for the flaws found in this product. The insurers are also responsible for the post claim underwriting of this product. If a claim is denied, it is the insurer denying the claim and not the bank. But who is getting the blame? The insurers make certain that the banks get the blame.

What are the flaws with mortgage insurance that can cost you a lot of money? Mortgage insurance sold directly by the banks is not portable. This does not apply to mortgage insurance sold by independent mortgage brokers. When mortgage insurance is not portable, it means that if you switch you mortgage to another bank; you will lose your mortgage insurance. If your health has changed you may be unable to get new insurance.

Mortgage insurance decreases with your mortgage amount. The lower the mortgage and the lower your mortgage insurance will be. If your health changes this is a very bad situation. While this is happening your premium does not decrease and it remains the same.

You are paying the same amount to buy less and less insurance.

You can't convert it to permanent insurance. Again if your health changes, the conversion feature is worth a lot of money.

On some mortgage insurance – the one sold by banks and not mortgage brokers – you cannot name a beneficiary. The bank is automatically the beneficiary. There are situations where it would be better not to repay your mortgage…

There is the issue of post claim underwriting; an issue which is often mentioned by the insurance industry and therefore publicized to make the banks look bad. All life insurance policies go through post claim underwriting whether it is mortgage or regular life insurance. Before paying a claim, an insurance company will check whether or not you have disclosed all of your health information. You just have to look at lawsuits involving many regular life insurance policies where the insurer refused to pay a claim following post claim underwriting.

The real issue is that when you buy mortgage insurance you are on your own to answer the questions on the application. Because they are not licensed in life insurance, the mortgage broker or employee of the bank cannot help you in answering correctly the questions found on the application. When you buy life insurance, the insurance agent will read the questions on the application to you and it is his job to ensure you understand these questions. If he does not do this, it is done over the phone by a paramedical company.

When you are on your own at a very stressful moment in your life, filling out a life insurance application by yourself, may not be the best idea. You are trying to process the fact you are buying a home. You are scared and it is easy to misread one of the questions. If you die, post claim underwriting will show the mistake you've made and the claim will be denied.

Mike, mortgage insurance is group insurance. Would you blame your employer for the insurer refusing to pay a claim?

Should you buy mortgage insurance? What do you think Mike? You don't know. The answer is yes. If you take a mortgage you should have insurance to cover this risk and liability immediately. You should not refuse to take that insurance in order to apply for real insurance.

Tip seventeen: You should take the mortgage insurance. A few months later, when you have moved in your house and you now feel comfortable being a home owner, you should contact a life insurance agent. Request a need analysis to determine what you need for insurance is. This insurance will not only cover your mortgage but it will also cover you income. You NEVER cancel the mortgage insurance until you have been approved with real life insurance and you have received the policy.

TERM INSURANCE vs. PERMANENT INSURANCE

You want to lose money when buying insurance, the easy way to do it is to buy permanent insurance. Mike, I am not arguing that term insurance is better than permanent insurance. When you consider all of the insurance needs of Canadians, considering the amount of premiums these Canadians can pay, permanent insurance is the last choice to consider.

For the fun of it and for my education, I like to ask my customers if they have insurance and what kind.

I was surprised to hear many people telling me that they have a pitiful amount of insurance such as $50,000 of permanent insurance. I asked these people how much they make in one year. The average income is about $30,000. We are not very rich around here...

Anyway, I am not an insurance agent, but I can still add two and two together. I believe that at a minimum these people need $300,000 of insurance which represents 10 years of income. This is a minimum. How did they end up with $50,000? This should not be happening. It's even illegal and prohibited by law.

Maybe it's cheaper...But when I asked how much they are paying,

I get as an answer, a number worth thousands of dollars when the $300,000 term insurance would only cost a few hundreds of dollars.

When I asked these people if they have other form of insurance such as critical illness or disability, their answer is negative. They can't afford it. They can barely pay the premium for their permanent insurance.

I met a lady recently. She had insurance with Desjardins Insurance. She was divorced with 2 young children. Her income was about $30,000 and she was struggling to make the payment on a $50,000 permanent insurance policy. If she was to die, what were her children going to do with $50,000? She could not even pay the premium. She was borrowing on her credit card to pay the premium. I told her it was wrong and she followed my advice to talk to a good insurance agent. The agent replaced the insurance with $200,000 term for a premium that was five times cheaper!!! The worst is that Desjardins Insurance made threats against the agent stating that the replacement was illegal and that they would the regulator to investigate him.

How can this be?

I've asked the question to a life agent. He told me that the law requires, when selling life insurance, that a need analysis be done. However it is not required by law that the need analysis be submitted with the life application to the insurer. As a result, insurers never asked for this legal document. Why?

Because it's extremely profitable for them...Think about it. They are only on the hook for a liability of $50,000 if the person dies while receiving 10 times more in premiums. We are talking thousands of dollars more in premiums. As for the agent, instead of receiving a small commission of a few hundreds of dollars, he will be receiving a commission of a few thousands of dollars. You have to know, that insurers front the commission on life policies. They pay up front, up to 1.5 to 2 times the premium selected under a permanent life policy.

Most of these permanent policies will lapse over time. Again it is a very profitable scenario for the insurers because they collected more premiums and they won't have to pay a death benefit.

The impact on families is disastrous. Imagine two families where the income earner dies. One family receives $50,000 and the other receives $300,000

Tip eighteen: You never buy life insurance without a proper need analysis. You buy all of the insurance you need, as shown on the need analysis, using term insurance. If after buying this term insurance, you have money left, you should consider critical illness and disability. If there is some money left after this, then you have a choice. You can transfer some of this term insurance into permanent insurance or instead buy long term care insurance. Only 1% of the population has money left after dealing with their life insurance need and critical illness need. I don't understand why so many people have permanent life insurance policies.

CHILDREN INSURANCE

If you want to buy permanent insurance, buy it on the life of your children. The best way to do this is to buy a small amount such as $25,000. By buying a whole life participating policy, you select the option of having the dividends paid by the policy to buy additional insurance. This could cost as low as $500 per year. Every year, your insurance will increase resulting in more dividends getting paid which will purchase more insurance.

Why would you do this? Isn't it a good idea to buy something that you will need when it is the cheapest? Everybody will need life insurance at one point. It is just a question of time. It is also just a question of time before you get a sickness that will impact your insurability negatively. When your child gets married and need life insurance to protect his family, will he be able to buy it? At what price? If you already bought the insurance, you don't have to worry.

Do you remember what I told you about the Fair Market Value of insurance? The fair market value of insurance issued on children is very high. If your child starts a business in the future, he could transfer the insurance to his business on a fair market value basis. What a great way to fund a startup business by saving a lot of income taxes...

I am talking here from experience Mike. I have a child and I bought a $50,000 policy for about $1,000 yearly premium. The policy is now ten year old and the amount of insurance is now about $250,000 and it has a cash value of about $10,000. I am putting $1,000 this year and the cash value will increase by $2,000 and the death benefit should increase by another $25,000. Not too bad a result for $1,000 a year.

My child will never have to buy insurance and I think this is worth a lot...

UNIVERSAL LIFE AS AN INVESTMENT

Mike, I will make it easy for you. Life insurance and in particular Universal Life is not an investment. It should never be used as a retirement savings vehicle. This is strictly an estate planning tool and you can't retire on it.

Too many people have lost money with buying Universal Life because there is nothing true about any of the representations made about this product. Everything is a lie. Universal Life allows you to accumulate tax free saving because the cash value is not subject to accrual taxation – this is a lie. The cash value shown on the illustration – this is a lie. Cash Values are totally fabricated. I could go on but someone wrote a book about it and it is called "Unraveling the Universal Life Scam" https://www.amazon.ca/Unraveling-Universal-Life-Richard-Proteau

Life settlement

While life insurance is not an investment it does not mean it does not acquire any value.

Life insurance is an asset and like any assets, it has many different values. The FMV of a life insurance policy is the amount that an informed third party dealing at arm's length would be willing to offer to purchase the life policy in question.

Normally to determine the FMV of a policy, a policy owner would hire an actuary to do the valuation. Usually the process would start with a pre-evaluation which is a rough estimate of the FMV. The cost is $250 to $500. This estimate is then used to decide whether there are any benefits in ordering a full valuation which usually cost around $2,500.

The FMV_Life App replaces the pre-evaluation which will save you time and money. The FMV_Life App provides an estimate of the value of the death benefit. However it does not include the value of any other guaranteed benefits such as interest guarantee, paid up additions... The values of such guarantees should be determined through a full evaluation.
https://play.google.com/store/apps/details?id=com.calculator.mrfmv1&hl=en

Mike you are asking if an evaluation has to be done by an actuary if you want to use the FMV of your policy.

The answer is negative. An actuary provides an actuarial evaluation of the policy. That evaluation may be different than what the FMV truly is. An actuary may not know what a third party will offer you for your policy. However it is usually recommended that such a valuation takes place as it easier for the policy owner to justify the FMV.

Why is the FMV of your policy important?

Because policy owners are unaware of the FMV, they are unable to choose the best form of settlement for their policies. As a result in the USA alone, policy owners mostly made of seniors lose $112 billion in life insurance benefits every year.

What is a life settlement?

There are many definitions of a life settlement. This has created a lot of confusion. Insurers have simplified a life settlement to the notion of a Viatical life settlement to discredit any forms of settlements outside of the forms of settlement they offer through the life policy contract. I believe it is wrong and that to protect consumers we have to change the discussion in order to view a life settlement from a comprehensive perspective.

A life settlement is the disposition, wholly or in part, of an interest in the property of a life insurance policy in favor of a third party for or without any forms of considerations.

There are two main types of life settlements and they are contractual life settlement and non-contractual life settlements.

Contractual Life Settlement

A contractual life settlement is the disposition of an interest in a policy, wholly or in part, under one of the provisions found in the life policy contract. In this case the third party who receives the interest in the policy is the insurer. There are 3 main types of Contractual life settlement;

1) Cash Value Settlement: This is the liquidation value of a policy whereby a policy owner liquidates his death benefit position in exchange for the cash value of the policy (CSV). We could state that in exchange of the CSV, the insurer regains the property of the death benefit. Usually the liquidation value (CSV) is inferior to the FMV and this is why liquidation is very profitable to the insurer.

2) Loan Settlement: Most life policy contract allows the policy owner to take a policy loan against the cash value of his policy without having to liquidate his death benefit position. Interest will accrue against the loan as per the interest rate stated in the contract. This rate would be currently a lot higher than current interest rates. Depending on the adjusted cost base of a policy, this loan may be taxable contrary to a loan made under a non-contractual life settlement.

3) Living Benefit (Disability and Critical illness): The Disability benefit is the payment of the CSV tax-free when the insured is faced usually with a total disability or a critical illness. The living benefit is different. When an insured is faced with an illness that has significantly decreased its life expectancy, the policy owner could request an advance on the death benefit. This was the insurers' response to justify their opposition to Viatical settlements. Sadly insurers have not honored their promise and have made the qualifications extremely difficult to meet in order to qualify for a living benefit. It is obvious!!! Insurers would prefer that the policy owner takes the CSV, lapsing the policy, instead of offering an advance on the death benefit.

Non – Contractual Life Settlement

A non-contractual life settlement is a settlement obtained outside of the contract with a third party that is usually not the insurer.

1) Leveraged settlement: This settlement involves using the life policy to secure one loan or series of loans by assigning the policy as collateral. The third party is a lender which is usually a bank. Sadly the banks are not willing to consider the full FMV of a policy and only loan on the CSV of the policy. This type of settlement is usually used to create additional retirement income.

2) Corporate settlement: This is a very important type of settlement and involves a transfer of ownership of a life policy between an individual and his corporation. The tax liability or tax benefit is based on the FMV of the policy and this is why an evaluation of the policy is highly recommended for this type of settlement. Usually there is a tax liability upon the transfer of a policy from a corporation to an individual. When the reverse is done, transferring a life insurance policy to a corporation, it can be a great way to move money out of the corporation tax free.

3) Family settlement: This should be the most common type of life settlement and the fact it is not, illustrates that advisors are not conserving life policies. Prior the cancellation of a policy, the policy owner should have a discussion about the FMV of his policy with his

family to see if one of the members of the family is willing to take over the policy by continuing paying premiums even if the cash value is withdrawn. This type of settlement can also be done on a Split Dollar basis as described below.

4) Charitable settlement: This type of settlement involves the donation of the life policy to a charity. Revenue Canada now allows the transfer to be done at Fair Market Value instead of at Cash Surrender Value. The financial decision of proceeding with the donation will depend whether or not the value of the charitable tax credit is greater than the after-tax value of the CSV.

5) Reverse loan settlement: This loan takes its origin from the Reverse Mortgage. The third party is usually a private lender who will accept to do a loan based on the death benefit and life expectancy of the insured. The policy is assigned as collateral and the policy owner retains the property of the life insurance. For provinces where this is considered trading and where trading is prohibited, this type of loan is still available. However the policy will not be directly assigned and a claim will instead exist against the estate. Since there is no change of ownership, there is no disposition, and therefore the amount received is not taxable or reduced by taxes.

6) Viatical settlement: This is an arrangement whereby the policy owner suffering from an illness is selling his life insurance policy to third part that is in the business of buying such life policies. There is a change ownership and it will trigger a disposition of the policy which may result in taxes. Also the amount of the FMV above the proceeds of disposition will also have to be included in the income of the policy holder. As a result, from a tax perspective it is the least advantageous of choices.

7) Split dollar settlement: This type or arrangement involves the splitting of a life insurance policy into two benefits, the death benefit and cash surrender value benefit with one of the benefit owned by the current policy owner and the other benefit transferred and owned by a third party under a rental or ownership agreement. Popular at issue of a policy, this type of settlement can also be put in place at anytime during the life of a life policy. This type of arrangement

could be combined with a family settlement or corporate settlement. For example, a policy holder would transfer on a rollover basis the death benefit of his policy to his investment corporation in exchange for the FMV but would retain the ownership of the CSV and the ability to further invest into the policy on a personal basis if for example the policy had an interest rate guarantee of 4%.

13 GROUP INSURANCE

> *Private group insurance is built on the basis of privatizing profits while socializing losses. It can only be profitable by denying Canadians insurance coverage based on where they live and where they work. As a society we have decided that a large part of our population will not be insured in order for companies to engage in the business of insurance. (The Poor Bartender)*

Private group insurance is the biggest hoax and scam devised to take advantage of the lack of knowledge of the public. If we wanted to solve the retirement crisis, the only way to do it, would be to improve the Canada Pension Plan. Public group insurance works. Private group insurance does not work unless you sacrifice a part of the population. For this sacrifice, the politicians have volunteered the poor, the disable, rural Canada... to privatize group insurance.

If we were to do away with private retirement, just the savings from the MERs, would increase the retirement benefits of Canadians by more than 40%.

To add to the injury, big corporations receive big tax incentives and welfare from the provincial and federal government. One of those companies is Bombardier. Because of this welfare paid from our taxes, employees of Bombardier have access to a pension plan. Bombardier's pension plan is subsidized by the taxes of those who do not have access to a pension plan. Is this right?

I'll repeat so you get it Mike. The creation of a retirement industry through the privatization of retirement can only be achieved by denying some Canadians access to a pension plan. It is not surprising if politicians have not volunteered to be part of this sacrifice. Instead they have voted for themselves one of the largest and most generous public pension plan.

The same principle applies to group health insurance. Why do we have public healthcare? It is public because we believe that access to healthcare can only be done on a cost efficient basis if it is available to all on an equal basis. Privatization of healthcare would be based on insuring those with good health (the good risk) while denying coverage to those who are sick (the bad risk); or letting the government take care of the bad risk (privatize the profit and socialize the loss).

No group plans whether it is private or public can survive if it is insuring only the bad risk. Insurance is a pool of risk. This pool must include the good and the bad. But this is not how group insurance works. By privatizing group insurance, the government has accepted the creation of pools of good risk while the bad risk because of health, geography and wealth is taken care by the government or simply ignored and denied access to insurance.

Then magically at age 65, the government states that we will take care of everyone. No more private plan because it is not profitable anymore for insurers to insure this risk. The insurers have made their profits and now the loss is passed on to the government. The only way to insure people that are 65 and over is to insure them when they were younger permitting you to set aside the required reserve to pay for the increased number of claims generated by that age group.

YOU CANNOT insure people that are over the age of 65 by relying on current revenues (without any reserves). This is financially impossible but the government has chosen to go down this route…

This is a good intro to group insurance Mike. What a scam! We need a good drink for this topic and I have chosen the Jack Rose.

A Jack Rose is a cocktail containing applejack, grenadine, and lemon or lime juice. It was popular in the 1920s and 1930s. It was mentioned in Ernest Hemingway's 1926 classic, The Sun Also Rises.

There are various theories as to the origin of the drink's name. The most interesting theory and the one I like the most is that the drink was named after the infamous gambler Bald Jack Rose. Jack Rose was a great liar. In July 13, 1912, a gambler by the name of Herman Rosenthal was called away from the bar of Times Square's Hotel Metropole. He was shot four times in the head. Jack Rose was the guy who put out the contract. A cop named Lieutenant Charles Becker of the NYPD's antigambling squad was accused of the murder. Rose was the star witness behind this accusation. Perjuring himself with a lot of enthusiasm and imagination, he accused this cop of this crime. This quickly became the trial of the century. Becker went to the chair which is telling you a lot about the death penalty.

The Jack Rose is a testament to this story. It's smooth and deeply deceptive. Sipping it, you can't tell if it contains liquor of any kind, not even the 2 ounces of applejack.

As for Jack Rose, all bad deeds get rewarded. At the end of the trial, gamblers started to bet that Rose would be murdered within a matter of days or weeks for acting as an informant. That did not happen. Rose was offered $1,000 a week to appear in vaudeville. He even received countless requests to lecture on crime. Later, Rose started speaking at churches preaching against gambling and other vices. He later went on to lecture U.S. troops against gambling. Who says there is no justice?

Health and Pharmacare

When you look at group insurance and health care, the discussion is about whether health is a social right or a private right. Health as a private right would be based on your wealth status....

It is interesting Mike, that as a society, we chose and embraced two different and opposite views. By establishing Universal Health Care, Canadians have stated that health is a social guaranteed right. So access to health care and hospitals is guaranteed to everyone and paid through our taxes. But then we decided that medication that is needed to ensure this health is not a guaranteed right and is in fact a private right.

Does this make sense to you? It does not and this is why each province has instituted Pharmacare where you will be certain to get the worst of a social plan and the worst of a private plan.

We have created a system where we have allowed the people who represent the good risk to go their own way and get their medication through private group insurance. For the people who represent the bad risk, we give them access to a social program that we call Pharmacare run by provincial governments. This gets even worst. When the people who represent the good risk become the bad risk because of aging, becoming unemployed, developing health issues, they are transferred to Pharmacare.

We have created a system where we privatize the good risk allowing insurers to make enormous profits. The insurers are faced with little risk since the losses have been socialized. This system can't work for us. Insurers love it. They make tremendous profits but it will bankrupt our society.

Sadly we all are going to pay for this. Mike you are just like me. Since we live in a rural area and since I am self employed and you work for a small business, we don't have access to private group insurance and we are forced into the Pharmacare social program which is a lousy program. The only way Pharmacare can work is by making certain we can't use it. My deductible is so high; it's about $5,000. This means Pharmacare is worthless to me.

Disability and Unemployment

Privatizing profit and socializing losses is the way big corporations make profit. Here is a great story for you. I had a few clients who worked for a call center named Convergys. This call center takes advantage of rural areas by exploiting its employees. It likes to attract these employees by capitalizing on the fact it is offering group insurance benefits.

As part of this group insurance, they had disability offered by Sun Life. Convergys practiced what I called employee clear cutting. The call center operated in a manner that was unhealthy and very stressful to its employees in order to fully exploit these employees. A lot of employees would simply quit but other who could not afford to lose their employment would get sick. As time passed, the call center would go through the local workforce until it would be unable to recruit new employees as this is an unsustainable commercial practice.

The call center would then close under the excuse that the contract was changed or cancelled. The call center would then move somewhere else. This is like clear cutting and it comes a point where the trees left are so far away that the operations must be moved. Replace trees with employees and you have the same thing.

Under stress many of the employees would be ordered by their doctor to get off work. These employees would then apply for their disability benefits offered by the Sun Life group insurance. In most cases, Sun Life would automatically decline to pay. These employees would instead go on disability under their unemployment insurance. It became so bad that the unemployment office stopped asking questions. You said Convergys and you were automatically accepted.

Think about it. The unemployment insurance is priced to be the second payor. Under this scheme it is now the first payor. Sun Life gets the premium for the disability insurance but never has to pay the claim in most cases. That's great profit. Instead it is you, me and everyone else who have to pay the claim. As far as Convergys, they don't care. The high level of disability does not impact the pricing of the insurance since most claims are simply denied. Convergys can continue promoting an unhealthy work environment to exploit employees without being forced to change these practices.

I had another client with Convergys. He had surgery and the doctor put him on 3 months rest to recover. The claim specialist at Sun Life called him stating that he should be able to work in less than two weeks. Imagine a claim specialist who thinks he knows better than a doctor. Instead the employee went on unemployment insurance. What a scam!

Mike, I have another story for you so that you understand what I am saying. There was this employee working at Manulife who had to go on disability because of changes that Manulife had introduced. The sole purpose of these changes was to reduce the number of employees no matter what. It was not important if these employees played a vital and critical function. This employee who was pretty senior tried to make it work. However when you go from 14 employees to 3 employees and the 11 employees who were let go were known to work well beyond regular hours, something had to give. Stress got to him and his health quickly deteriorated. He even suffered the loss of his short term memory. His doctor had to intervene by putting him off work.

Manulife kept calling him everybody asking him when he was going to get back to work. They even insinuated he was faking it. Finally they requested that he went to see a specialist Manulife selected. When this doctor selected by Manulife met the employee, he was so appalled by what he diagnosed that he doubled the medication of the employee. Still Manulife kept pressuring him to come back to work calling him every day. These claims specialist were very good. They played on his pride. They knew he saw his health problems as a failure and Manulife preyed on this. So imagine if Manulife is willing to do this to one of its own employee, ask yourself what it is capable to do. Would you trust them with your disability insurance?

Self insurance

This is one option the group insurance industry is keeping secret. Why do you need to insure an event that is guaranteed to happen and will happen on a regular basis? Insurance is to insure an unpredictable risk…

You know how much each employee will spend on regular medication and you how much you will have to pay as an employer. Why would you insure this? It is not a risk. This expense will have to be paid no matter what. The choice is to pay the cost of the medication directly to the employee or use an intermediary which will be the insurer in this case. However if you use an insurer as an intermediary, the expense will be grossed up by 40% to 50% to pay for commission, administration and profits.

Truly, the only insurable risk is that an employee has an unforeseen sickness which requires special and costly medication. This is the risk. It cannot be foreseen and predicted. This is what you want to insure.

So do you insure or self-insure? The grossed up cost of the group insurance which is called the premium will always be higher than the expected benefit. Grossing up the cost of insurance is very profitable for the insurer. Many techniques are used mainly at renewal to increase the premium. A technique the insurers often use is to use 11 months of premium and 12 months of claim in addition to unapproved claims. This always creates a deficit which is used as a justification to increase the premium.

Mike we can put it this way. If there are no profits to be delivered to shareholders and expenses to recover, the premiums associated with a risk would be equal to the probability of the event to occur multiplied by the size of the loss. This would be the net cost of insurance for the coverage. Such cost of insurance is not realistic. The true cost of insurance which is called the premium will always be higher. The difference is referred as the 'load factor' and this represents a lot of profit for insurers.

Buying insurance for a known risk and a risk guaranteed to happen will always be a losing proposition. Whether you buy the insurance becomes a question of convenience. You are not buying insurance. You are buying the administration. If you can't pay for the employee's cost of medication you won't be able to pay the insurance premium which will be higher. The only solution is to offer no coverage at all.

The catastrophic loss is the cost of medication spiraling out of control. This is what should be insured and there is insurance available for this. You won't hear it from an advisor because they will be losing a lot of commission.

For example, the employees of a business spend in average $100,000 per year in medication. The business could set $100,000 aside to pay for this expense. If the business decides to purchase group insurance instead, the premium would be around $150,000. Why would you do this? It is a question of administration.

You could set aside the $100,000 and insure the risk that medication will rise above the $100,000. Let's say the cost for this insurance is $25,000. What would the advisor recommend? The solution where he will get commissioned on $25,000 or the solution where he will get commissioned on $150,000? What is best for you? Paying $125,000 or $150,000?

In a recent Globe and Mail article "The lowdown on insurance salesmen and warranty peddlers" Moshe Milevsky writes that you should "Insure only events that have a potentially disruptive impact on your lifestyle and only if they have a relatively low probability of occurring." He is absolutely right.

Mike I have a story for you. It is named the Cuggia Story and it is a story of a man the government and the financial industry tried to destroy because he found a way to deliver cheap group insurance. He was a threat to the insurance industry and he had to go.

Mr. Cuggia worked in the group insurance industry and he was a very intelligent fellow. It did not take long for him to understand that the way group insurance was sold was wrong because it was built on discriminating against less advantageous groups in our society. He particularly did not like that small businesses or small employers could not get group insurance or had to pay much higher premiums than anybody else.

So he decided to do something about it. If the insurer was able to charge more by discriminating and creating smaller pools of risks, he came up with the idea to charge less by creating bigger pools of risks. He did this when he introduced his product "All For One". The idea was simple. Why not pool all small businesses together and treat them like a big employer even if they were separate businesses. It worked. He was able to reduce group insurance premiums by 25% to 40%. He was a little bit like the Tucker of the insurance industry…

It's not easy being a visionary. It's hard to be innovative, to challenge the established order while the bureaucrats are always ready to accuse you of fraud because you are unable to describe the route and every turn you will make; interpreting this as a deception.

Mr. Cuggia became the target of the AMF (Quebec regulator). The AMF wrote several complaints against him and found business owners willing to sign these complaints in exchange for receiving more than $25,000 each. These complaints stated that Mr. Cuggia was their agent and that he had lied about the premium of their group insurance. Under the interrogation of Cuggia's lawyer, these people finally recanted these accusations. They had never met Mr. Cuggia. They did know who he was. Mr. Cuggia is now fighting hard to have the Court of Appeal review this new testimony showing perjury. The question is whether the Court of Appeal will accept to view this as a legal question and not as a new fact (which cannot be the subject of an appeal).

JUSTICE IS NOT ABOUT RIGHT OR WRONG. STOP BELIEVING WHAT YOU ARE SEEING ON TV. JUSTICE IS ABOUT PROCEDURES. PROCEDURAL LAW TRUMPS THE TRUTH.

Through Mr. Cuggia's product we rediscover the principle of the universality of insurance. The more people have insurance the cheaper it will be. This is not what insurers want. They want profits. They want to charge more while reducing the possibility of claims. There are a lot of profits in practicing insurance discrimination. The greater the discrimination in a pool of risks, the greater the profits the insurance company can make and the greater the cost to society. This appetite for profits, the greed of insurance companies has perverted the noble and original principle and purpose of insurance.

Mr. Cuggia showed this and he paid dearly for his vision.

RICHARD PROTEAU

14 REGULATORY ENVIRONMENT

Barely 5% of licensing fees and taxes taken from the financial industry are used to enforce regulations and protect consumers. 0% of the fines imposed on infractions committed by advisors are used to compensate their victims. Fraud and exploitation of the consumers are very profitable to the government since it extracts its pound of flesh from the wrong doings of advisors. The regulators are the gatekeepers and guardian of this system which is called "Regulated Fraud" (The Poor Bartender)

Monkey Gland is a classic drink from the 1920s that balances gin and fresh orange juice with a splash of Absinthe and a little pomegranate grenadine. It is possible to enjoy this cocktail even if you don't have much of a taste for gin. The strange name does not have anything to do with what we will be discussing. However with the strange story behind the name of this drink, I had to make one for you.

Harry McElhone, the famed proprietor of Harry's New York Bar in Paris, created this drink. Its name was inspired by experiments made by the surgeon Serge Voronoff in the arena of male enhancement. I don't know what was in the mind of McElhone but he had a dark sense of humor. You had to be weird to name a drink on a process where you implant slivers of freshly vivisected Monkey testicle into the Scrota of elderly Frenchmen. Voronoff believed that testosterone was the key to a long and healthy life. For $5,000 you could access this fountain of youth. They did not have Viagra in those days…

THE POOR BARTENDER

To make this drink, you use 1½ oz. gin, 1½ oz. fresh orange juice, 1 tsp. grenadine, 1 tsp. simple syrup and 1 tsp. absinthe. You shake well over ice cubes in a shaker, strain into a chilled cocktail glass.

As a consumer, you should consider the regulator as the enemy. This is the sad truth Mike. The regulators are not there to protect us. They are there to protect an orderly system where we can be exploited through outrageous fees and where those fees are shared by the industry and the government.

For protecting this system, the government gets to take licensing fees, premium taxes and HST on financial products. Our savings are a major source of government revenues. When the government fails to protect us, it goes after the advisors who took advantage of their clients collecting millions in fines. None of the victims get any of that money. The victims are on their own and have to use common law or the civil code to collect what they have lost. Considering the cost of accessing the justice system, most victims can't.

So here you have it. If you lose money to a so called advisor, your only recourse is pretty much this Monkey Gland you are drinking right now.

There is a war being fought in the financial industry and this war will irrevocably show on which side of the fence the regulators are sitting on.

Too many investors assume financial advisers have a duty to act in their best interests. Again Mike they are lying to you right from the start. They are not financial advisers. They are sales representatives. Their only duty is to make sure that the product they are selling to you is suitable. There do not owe you a fiduciary duty which is a very high standard to meet. Sales representatives are always in a conflict of interest. Their goal is to make commission. Sales representative are not required to recommend the best product. For the moment the product is suited to the need, they have done their job. Under the fiduciary duty, they would be obligated to recommend the best product.

This is why the financial industry is fighting so hard against the disclosure of fees and commissions which they believe would ultimately result into a fee based system instead of a commission based system. Under a fee based system, the financial institutions lose control of the representative which now owes a fiduciary duty to the client paying the fee. What is the difference between an MER of 2.65% with an embedded commission of 1% and a MER of 1.65% where the client pays a fee of 1% to the advisor? It is the same thing except who controls the advisor and what duty the advisor is required to provide.

I think that this fight will continue on and on. While this fight rages on, consumers will continue to be exploited. So what do you to protect yourself Mike? The answer is simple really. If you use a sales representative disguised as a financial advisor, make him sign an advisory contract creating that fiduciary duty for the cost of $1. The advisor will still be able to collect his commission but you can impose a fiduciary duty on him. I have a copy of such contract which you can reproduce if you want.

SAMPLE CONTRACT: THIS SAMPLE CONTRACT SHOULD NOT BE CONSTRUED AS BEING LEGAL ADVICE. IT IS PROVIDED FOR THE PURPOSE OF INFORMATION ONLY. IT IS THE SOLE RESPONSABLILITY OF THE USER OF THIS AGREEMENT TO CHOOSE WHETHER OR NOT TO SEEK LEGAL ADVICE AND TO ESTABLISH WHETHER OR NOT THIS AGREEMENT IS LEGAL AND BINDING IN THEIR CURRENT LEGAL JURISDICTION.

The undersigned, _____, [hereinafter "Client"] hereby appoints _____[hereinafter "Advisor"] to act as a financial advisor in accordance with the following terms and conditions of this agreement [hereinafter "Agreement"] in supplement to the legal obligations created by the Advisor being licensed in mutual funds/insurance in the province of _____as a sales representative/insurance agent.

Terms and Conditions

1. **General Conditions and Responsibilities**

The Agreement creates a fiduciary duty, arising expressly from this contract, on the part of the Advisor towards the Client in addition to the suitability duties and requirements owed to the Client established under the provincial licenses held by the Advisor. In signing this Agreement, the Advisor accepts to provide financial advice to the Client by acting in the best interest of the Client and by putting the Client's interests ahead of his own at all times. Under this fiduciary duty, the Advisor must provide advice that he views as being the best for the Client and in addition must also adhere to the following duties:

2. **Duty of Care:** The Advisor must exercise due care (prudence and reasonableness) when acting on behalf the Client. He must employ reasonable care to avoid misleading the Client. He must have a reasonable basis for his advice.

3. **Duty of Loyalty:** The Advisor must act in the best interest of the Client. He must place the interest of the Client above his own. He must avoid conflicts of interest, or if they cannot be avoided altogether, obtain the Client informed consent in regards to the existence of the conflict of interest after full disclosure of this conflict of interest. He must not compromise the best execution of the financial advice provided. He must not use the Client's assets and information for his own benefit or the benefit of others.

4. **Duty of Obedience:** The Advisor must adhere to the terms of any laws governing the regulation of his licensed activities in addition to the obligations arising from this contract. He must follow any instructions or guidelines provided by the Client.

5. **Duty to Act in Good Faith:** The Advisor must act honestly toward the Client and with utmost good faith. He must treat the Client fairly.

6. **Duty of Disclosure:** The Advisor must provide full and fair disclosure of all material facts to the Client. He must not mislead the Client. The Advisor must informed the Client within 48 hours of any changes in the status of his licenses or being found guilty of an infraction under any regulations applying to the licenses he has.

7. **Duty of confidentiality:** The Advisor must protect the confidentiality of the information of the Client. Prior storing the information of the Client on the web, cloud or with any third party, for any purposes including need analysis and financial planning, the

Advisor must secure the consent of the Client. This consent does not waive the responsibility of the Advisor for the security of the Client's confidential information in the event of a breach of security at the third party's site.

8.   **Compensation:** This Agreement does not modify the way the Advisor is compensated under the form of commissions paid on financial products sold to the Client and paid through an investment dealer/ insurer/MGA. The Advisor agrees to inform the Client of any changes to his commission scale associated with the sale of a financial product and to disclose any other money and other non-monetary incentives that the Advisor could receive upon selling a financial product to the Client.

9.   **Termination:** This Agreement shall be valid until terminated by Client or Advisor. This Agreement may be terminated at any time upon written notice by either party and termination will be become effective upon receipt of such notice. Upon termination of this Agreement, the Advisor shall have no further obligations to provide any advice. Upon termination it shall be Client's exclusive responsibility to issue any financial instructions in regards to his financial situation.

Upon termination of this agreement, for any life policies including segregated funds and annuities, the Advisor shall relinquish any rights to receiving servicing or renewal commission payable on the life policies whether this commission is vested or not.

This Agreement shall also be terminated upon the Advisor ceasing to be licensed for mutual funds/insurance in the province where this Agreement was signed. The modality of the termination is listed in the Cancellation/suspension of the license provision of this agreement.

10.   **Cancellation/suspension of license:** Upon having his mutual fund license suspended or cancelled, the Advisor has 48 hours to inform the Client of this cancellation or suspension. The Advisor must arranged for a suitable mutual fund licensed Advisor within 2 weeks of the suspension or cancellation to take over the accounts and investments under the responsibility of the Advisor.

Upon having his life license suspended or cancelled, the Advisor has 48 hours to inform the Client of this cancellation or suspension. The Advisor must arrange for a suitable life licensed Advisor to take over the life policies including annuities and segregated funds under the responsibility of the Advisor within two weeks of the suspension of cancellation. The Advisor must arrange for the annual remuneration of the new Advisor with such remuneration not being greater than the annual value of the renewal and service commission associated with the policy or policies of the Client. In the event that the advisor does not arrange for a suitable life licensed to take over the servicing of the Client's life policies, the Client has the right to select a new life licensed advisor with the Advisor relinquishing all rights associated with being the agent of record including any owed or future vested commission payable on the life policies of the Client.

In exchange for the Advisor acting as a financial advisor under the terms of this agreement, the Client accepts to pay the Advisor a fee of $1 dollar.

Signed in   **Date:**
Client: **Advisor:**

The financial industry is unable to provide an answer to one question. Considering the volatility of the equity markets and interest rates being at its lowest, is it possible for a sales representative to provide advice that has any embedded value? When considering the low returns that most regular investments provide, is the MER of most mutual funds eating away at these low returns. Remember Mike, you don't get to be paid first. The fund manager and the advisor have first crack at your investment.

Saving money on MERs and commission will probably determine if the return on your investment will be positive or negative.

The whole system is based on you paying for sales recommendation disguised as sales advice without you being able to determine the value of this advice. I have a story for you Mike. This is the story of a fisherman that often comes to my bar.

Just yesterday I was talking to James and he gave me permission to tell his story. James is a lobster fisherman and a captain in Pubnico, Nova Scotia. When lobster season ends, he then goes crabbing. He has been doing this since the age of 12 and the stories he can tell about the fishing industry…

We were talking about money and I mentioned how important it was not to lose money when dealing with the financial industry. His reaction was priceless.

"This is so true," he said. "I've tried investing. I gave $135,000 to my financial advisor working at Investors Group. One day my financial advisor shows up at my door."

"Great news," he said. "You've made 18% this year."

I looked at him pondering what the good news was about. "I give you $135,000 about 10 years ago. Since last year I was down 20% and now I've made 18% this year, I should be about break even; I should have around $135,000 which is the amount that I invested in the first place... What is the good news?"

"That's impossible," my advisor answered. He was not even aware of how my investment did over 10 years...

"Well check it out then" And he did and to his discomfort he found out I was right. He took his retirement after this. It feels very nice for me to have contributed to his retirement while I continue working for my mine. Anyway I received a notice from Investors Group telling me I had a new investment advisor and that they were coming to see me.

So a car pulls in the driveway. I'm working in the back on some fishing gear with my buddy when we see two people going to the front door.

"Who is this?" he asked

"Probably my new investment advisor."

"But I recognized the girl. She just finished vocational school to become a hairdresser."

That was it for me. I pulled my money out and this was the last time I invested. I now invest all of my money in my fishing boats. If I lose 20% of my money I know why and understand why. Before when I lost 20% nobody told me anything and nobody told me why. Now I have these boats which are worth a lot of money and I am buying a new boat this year. All cash! Everybody thinks I am nuts including my ship builder. "I should borrow instead" they say. Well this is my answer to them: **"IF I AM SMART ENOUGH TO MAKE THE MONEY I AM SMART ENOUGH TO LOOK AFTER IT"**

Mike we have to wonder about the purposes of the laws. Are these laws there to protect us or are these laws there to give us the belief we are protected so that we let our guard down? Don't ask any questions and accept to buy investments where we will be paying fees that we should normally not accept. I'll give you an example. In Quebec there is a simple law. You cannot use and call yourself a financial advisor. This is what is called a prohibited title. How many sales representatives accept to follow this law? The answer is amazing; one out three representatives. This is 12,000 advisors over 36,000 who choose to break the law. The Quebec regulator knows about it. Do you think they are enforcing the law? No… Which laws will they enforce? Which law will the advisor believe he has to follow? Anyway why do we have laws that are not enforced and not followed? The only answer possible is to make the consumer feel secured.

It is quite a system really. Sales representatives state that you should not buy a financial product directly from a manufacturer. They state that by using them this protect the consumers because they have what is called error and omission insurance. If we use an intermediary and an error is committed, the consumers will be protected since this risk is insured. What a bunch of baloney…

They are not telling you that in their error and omission insurance contract there is a clause which states that gross negligence is not covered. However what is gross negligence? It can be anything! The error and omission insurer can easily denied the claim and if you want to be compensated you are back to going to court which most victims cannot do. Does the regulator and financial industry use this gap in the insurance error and omission to their advantage? The answer is yes. The perfect example is the case of a big fraudster in Quebec named Thibault.

Quebec, unlike any other provinces, has a fund that is supposed to compensate victims of fraud. It is controlled by the regulator and this is a conflict of interest. The existence of this fund is used to convince consumers of the necessity of using a licensed representative.

Thibault as a licensed sale representative lied on various life insurance applications. He declared that his clients had a large income in order to cash in on large commission that these large insurance policies generated; with premiums that these clients could not afford. Thibault falsified the insurance applications. This is fraud but the Quebec regulator did not want the fund to pay any compensation. Instead the regulator deemed that Thibault's actions were negligence. That's right Mike! You heard me right! Lying is now negligence. The regulator therefore told the victims it could not compensate them as the fund only covers acts of fraud. Instead they should make a claim under the error and omission insurance of Thibault. The insurance company did not want to pay either and decided to state that falsifying an insurance application was a gross negligence. They refused to pay the claim on that basis.

While Quebec has a fund to cover fraud; some other provinces use an ombudsman to resolve consumer issues. However the financial industry and its lobbyists feel that this ombudsman (OBSI) favors investors. In 2015, 65% of the cases where OBSI made a decision were resolved in favor of the firms in the industry. Only 219 cases went in favor of investors with slightly less than the $4.7 million that the ombudsman suggested be paid to the victimized investors.

Despite this the industry is not happy. Can you believe it Mike? These people and institutions have no moral or ethics. If this was the case they would respect the decisions of OBSI. How can they claim they are acting in our best interest and that we need them?

This gets worst when you understand that the money awarded by OBSI to investors as a form of compensation for the wrongdoings of advisors is only a suggestion. OBSI' suggestion is not enforceable. The firms can refuse to pay and they do it often because there are no consequences associated with their refusal. They can still continue to do business as usual. These are firms such as Toronto-based investment dealer Octagon Capital Corp. which refused to follow OBSI's recommendation that Octagon compensate an aggrieved investor to the tune of $181,339; or an Ontario based mutual fund dealer, W.H. Stuart and Associates (WHS) which declined to comply with a $41,066 compensation recommendation.

When you are dealing with a licensed representative who is marketing and positioning himself as an advisor, this is who you are really dealing with.

15 TFSA VERSUS RRSP

When we review the advice that the financial industry is giving in relation to choosing between a RRSP and TFSA, this is when we realize how many professionals in this industry don't know what they are talking about. (The Poor Bartender)

Well Mike, this is almost the last chapter before I do the big reveal and share with you how you should invest money for retirement if you don't want to lose money. But again you don't discuss such things while being dry and thirsty. I'll make you a Fog Cutter to help you cut through the fog obscuring the choice between a RRSP and a TFSA.

While the Fog Cutter is not a well known drink it is enjoying an increase in popularity. Victor "Trader Vic" Bergeron created this drink decades ago. Now Martin Cate, owner of Forbidden Island Tiki Lounge in Alameda, California is responsible for its new popularity. He likes this drink so much that he put the drink's name on his car's license plate.

There was a battle in those days. It was between Don the Beachcomber and Trader Vic and they were fighting for supremacy over the "Tiki Cocktails" during this era. By creating the Fog Cutter, Trader Vic won the battle and some say even the war. Vic even created special mugs for the drink and I wish I had one because they are now worth a small fortune. Trader Vic liked to say "Fog Cutter Hell, after two of these you won't even see the stuff". Maybe this was true of the San Francisco Bay Area but he hasn't been in the

Maritimes... Here it will take you at least three of those to see through our fog.

After everything I said to you in the last few days, your head is likely a little foggy tonight. Well here to the words of another: "With the fog cutter, experience shows that the first one cuts through the fog, while the second one cuts through any remaining coherence." Here's to the crazy world of financial services...

But be careful. The Fog Cutter is a strong drink. It has 2 ounces freshly squeezed orange juice, 1 ounce freshly squeezed lemon juice, 1/2 ounce Orgeat syrup, 1 1/2 ounces white rum, 1/2 ounce gin, 1/2 ounce brandy and 1/2 ounce Amontillado sherry.

The Wealthy Barber had a long discussion already about the choice between saving into a RRSP versus a TFSA. As you know Mike the TFSA is a tax-free savings account. This mean you put money that has been taxed and it can grow tax-free in this account. When you want it or at retirement, you can make withdrawals without having to pay any taxes.

With an RRSP, the money that is going in the RRSP is money that has not been taxed. This is how it is supposed to work but this is not how income taxation really works. As a result, most people contribute money that has been taxed in a RRSP and it is only at the end of the year, when they do their income taxes, that the taxes that should have been saved is refunded and applied to the income taxes that you owe or paid back to you if you don't owe anything.

Most people don't like the RRSP because taxes are deferred only. The government becomes your retirement partner waiting patiently for its share of the bounty. When the money is withdrawn from the RRSP, the government will get part of it. Most people don't like this at all.

Most people cannot fully use these two products to build their retirement. They don't have enough money and they have to choose one over the other. Which one is the best?

Some people believe the TFSA is the mirror image of an RRSP. However with the TFSA you contribute after-tax dollars while you contribute pre-tax dollars with the RRSP. Mike, I want you to listen very carefully to this because it is amazing how people don't understand this. With an RRSP, people put too much emphasis on the tax refund. In fact this is the fault of the investment industry which has used our greed against us to promote the sales of RRSPs.

A RRSP tax refund is not guaranteed. It depends on how much taxes you owe when you file your income tax. If you owe $1,000 and the RRSP contribution reduces your taxes by $400, there will be no refund. Taxes owed will decrease to $600. Often, we contribute to a RRSP from after-tax dollars and it is only when we file our income tax that this contribution is transformed into a pre-tax contribution through a tax adjustment which may or may not create a tax refund. The tax refund is a potential result; it is not the process itself.

For both the RRSP and TFSA, once the money is in these plans, it will grow free of tax. However when you withdraw the money from the RRSP, you will have to add the RRSP withdrawal to your income which may or may not generate additional income taxes. With the TFSA, the withdrawals are not added to your income and will therefore be tax-free.

This is a chart usually used by everyone (including the Wealthy Barber) to compare TFSA against RRSP

	TFSA	versus	RRSP
Pre-tax Income	$1,000		$1,000
Tax	$ 400		N/A
Net contribution	$ 600		$1,000
Value 20 years later @ 6% growth	$1,924		$3,207
Tax upon withdrawal (40%*)	N/A		$1,283
Net withdrawal	$1,924		$1,924

* The marginal tax rate — the rate of tax charged on the last dollar of income

Basically, this shows that if your tax rate is the same when the contribution is made to the tax rate when the withdrawal is made, the

TFSA is the perfect mirror of an RRSP. Both products will deliver the same results. If your tax rate at the time of withdrawal is greater than the tax rate at contribution, then the TFSA is a better option.

The problem with this comparison is that an entry is missing. Mike, do you remember the story of Henry who worked more to find out he was making less? He started to understand this when he noticed that making more income reduces your government benefits. This principle is not accounted in the TFSA/RRSP comparison.

When you make a contribution to a TFSA, it does not reduce your income. If you are making $40,000 and you contribute $1,000 to a TFSA, your net income will still be $40,000. If you had made the same $1,000 contribution to a RRSP, your net income would now be $39,000. This means that government benefits would be calculated on $39,000 instead of $40,000. Since most government benefits such as children benefits or tax rebates are clawed back based on income, you would qualify for more benefits if your income was $39,000. The comparison should account for this:

	TFSA	versus	RRSP
Pre-tax Income	$1,000		$1,000
Decrease in government benefits	$ 400		$0
Tax	$ 400		N/A
Net contribution	$ 200		$1,000
Value 20 years later @ 6% growth	$641		$3,207
Tax upon withdrawal (40%*)	N/A		$1,283
Net withdrawal	$641		$1,924

Now we see that the TFSA is not the mirror of the RRSP. The Wealthy Barber was not entirely right!

What we find Mike, is that for the TFSA to be better, your tax upon withdrawal would have to be higher than 80%. What is the likelihood for this?

A lot of people state that your TFSA is better than RRSP because withdrawals from a TFSA would not result in the claw back of benefits such as Old Age Security pension, Guaranteed Income Supplement and other means-tested government benefits. This is true. So another line is needed to account for the claw back of benefits at retirement.

	TFSA versus	RRSP
Pre-tax Income	$1,000	$1,000
Decrease in benefits	$ 400	$0
Tax	$ 400	N/A
Net contribution	$ 200	$1,000
Value 20 years later @ 6% growth	$641	$3,207
Tax upon withdrawal (40%*)	N/A	$1,283
Gross withdrawal	$641	$1,924
Benefits claw backs at retirement	$0	$???
Net Withdrawal	$641	$???

* the marginal tax rate — the rate of tax charged on the last dollar of income

How do you solve this comparison for the benefits that will be clawed back at retirement? You can calculate the amount of benefits that you will lose today because of a TFSA contribution. However you cannot predict or know the amount of claw backs that a RRSP withdrawal will generate at retirement. Will there be a Guaranteed Income Supplement in 20 years? How will it work? Nobody knows...

Lucky for us mathematics can be so simple. We can calculate a breakeven point. In our example, based on the loss of benefits today, the RRSP claw backs at retirement would have to be 40%, increasing your tax rate above 80% for the TFSA to become better. Then it becomes a question of probability. The higher the claw back rate, the less likely this will happen.

When doing an analysis you have to account for everything; every penny. I totally disagree with the Wealthy Barber that the impact of the tax refund can be ignored because people just spend it. Imagine if you ran a business where you ignore some of your sales in your analysis by not including it in your income statement because you are just going to spend it? This is not done...

16 EDUCATION

Mike, education is part of financial planning. One of the best investments is yourself. However it is important to know whether you are investing in knowledge or you are investing in skills. Knowledge makes us a better person. However it is skills that make you attractive in the marketplace.

Considering the high cost of education, it is important to understand this. Universities focus on knowledge and you pay a high price for this knowledge. So here is a story for you. No drink this time…

The next bubble – the Education Bubble – when will it burst?

Take advantage of very low interest rates and get yourself an education, they say… It seems a cure to heal the economy. It seems a great way to finance economic growth. Better educated workforce means student getting higher paying jobs, living their nest, establishing their nest… As a result, we have seen in the US, student debt almost triple (in trillions) in the last 10 years; fuelling the price of education; saddling students with debt; avoiding having them on welfare.

I hate divergence when there should be convergence. Some see it as a money opportunity. What I see is a fundamental problem where either I don't know something or someone is playing a trick on me. When such divergence occurs, there has to be a loser and a winner.

And here we are. Students have not left the nest. They are not getting these high paying jobs. They are surviving on minimum wage or part time jobs... If the economy has improved it has more to do with the intervention of the Feds than Corporate.

In fact what has corporate been doing in the US? Corporate must be busy since their amount of borrowing has increased 1.5 times in the last 10 years. However I am unable to see the trickle of this money through the US economy. So where did the money go?

Well the borrowing of cheap money has been used to prop up the price of shares by using this borrowed money to pay dividends or share buybacks generating large pay bonuses. This basically means businesses have not been investing in their business for long term growth or any growth at all. It's all artificial. In other words you should watch your mutual fund returns very closely if interest rates go up significantly...

What will happen when interest rise again? Will these companies have the earnings to cover their debt position? If the corporate debt bubble burst, its impact on the student debt bubble will have the impact of a nuclear bomb in the same way the mortgage bubble destroyed homeowners.

And again the same choice will present itself. Is the government going to bail out corporate or will it bail out the students? Will the government make the same type of choice when it had to choose between the banks and the homeowners?

As a result, I am bearish on education and this is what I explained to my son as he is trying to decide what he will do now that he has completed high school. So I went to a career fair with him to talk with business owners, the real business owners who own small businesses; who don't borrow to prop up share price; who invest in their business because they care about their business and I started to ask questions. Here is my conversation with one business owner of a tech company.

Would you recommend to my son that he get a University Computing degree?

He shook his head negatively. "No."

"Why?" I asked.

"Because I would not hire him."

"Why?"

"Because I don't need educated employees, I need skilled employees. Come to me with a university degree in computing and I won't hire you – come to me showing me that you have the skill to do Word Press development and you are hired right on the spot– and he proceeded to give me a list of web sites with distance education and courses that he would recognized where you could get the skills he needed at a fraction of the cost of a University degree."

So education/University cost is rising; student debt is rising and business owners don't feel that this overpriced education is equipping the students with the skills they need. This is a definition of a bubble (inflated prices with deflated values).

I said to my son: "It's up to you but I would do the smart thing not the educated thing…"

17 BEWARE OF THE PROPHETS

Investing can be scary. It is easy to search for the magical solution. It is then that you become the prey of a financial prophet. If this happens, you will lose all of your money. Now Mike I am going to have a beer with you to discuss this. This is important stuff...

The financial prophet is someone very intelligent and who is very knowledgeable about economics. I'll play the role of the prophet. I will tell you that the US economy will be facing a crisis. Corporate debt has risen from 5 trillion to 8 trillion in the last 10 years. However corporations have not borrowed money to invest in their businesses in order to create growth and increase earnings. They have borrowed money to pay dividends and to do share buy backs in order to prop up their share price which explains why the S&P 500 has increased to its highest level when it should be moving in the opposite direction. This speculation has all been fueled by the ability of corporations to borrow cheap money.

So far everything I said is entirely true. It can be easily checked. Now that the facts are stated I have to create fear and urgency. What if interest rates rise? The corporations not having increased its earnings won't be able to service the debt. Bankruptcies will rise and the market will crash bursting the corporate loan bubble.

What can push interest rates up? So far the United States has been able to literally print money because of its access to low cost of borrowing. The US is running an incredible trade deficit. If we view the US dollar as a product, then this changes the entire picture. The US is able to finance its standard of living because of the existence of the petrodollar meaning that all transactions for oil must be made in US dollars. This creates a demand for US Treasuries which provides liquidities and offset this trade deficit.

Now this is about to all come down. Russia, Iran and China are waging a war on the petrodollar. The perfect storm is coming and lucky for you I can tell you exactly what to do to protect yourself from this financial Armageddon which usually will involve very risky investing such as options trading, buying gold, speculating on currencies but don't worry I have a system and if you buy into it, there are no risks.

Again this is all true. If the petrodollar ceases to exist, interest rates in the US will rise significantly. However no one can predict if this will happen because what is going to happen will not be driven by market forces but by political forces. A system to make money out of this does not exist. The system is about how to make money out of you and your fear. Stay away from these scams and the financial prophets.

TIP: "NOBODY WOULD IN THEIR RIGHT MIND SHARE AN EASY WAY TO GET RICH SCHEME THAT WORKS BY SHARING OR SELLING IT TO OTHERS. THIS IS NOT HOW GREED WORKS!"

18 SECRET TO NOT LOSING MONEY

At its most basic level, a Manhattan is a cocktail made with whiskey, vermouth, and bitters. Rye whiskey is the most traditional choice. Probably because there were many distilleries in New York. With the advent of Prohibition, Canadian whiskey became popular. It was the only thing available. Today any and all kinds of whiskey are used. This includes bourbon, and even brandy.

In regards to vermouth and the bitters, a Manhattan was made with sweet vermouth and Angostura bitters. Now dry vermouth and varying kinds of bitters are sometimes used. Maraschino cherries are also thrown into the drink for garnish. It's common to serve a Manhattan in a martini glass, lowball, or even a coupe; either straight or on the rocks.

In 1908, the Manhattan was named differently. It was called the Brooklyn Cocktail. There are two stories about the origin of this cocktail. The first story is that it was invented in the 1870's at the New York City's Manhattan Club. In this story, Lady Randolph Churchill, mother to Winston Churchill, was the host of a party thrown in honor of Samuel J. Tilden who was the presidential candidate at the time. A guest at the party named Dr. Iain Marshall started making Manhattans for the other guests and it was a success. It was so popular that people used the name of the club where the drink was created to order it.

The second story came from William F. Mulhall, a bartender who worked at the famous Hoffman House for more than 30 years. In the 1880s, he mentioned that: "the Manhattan cocktail was invented by a man named Black, who kept a place ten doors below Houston Street on Broadway in the 1860s" claiming that it was "probably the most famous drink in the world in its time."

This is why I'm using the Manhattan as a drink for what we will be discussing. Like the Manhattan there are two stories to investing.

To make a Manhattan, I usually used the classic recipe which is 2 oz rye whiskey, 1/2 oz dry vermouth, 2-3 dashes Angostura bitters, Maraschino cherry and/or lemon peel, for garnish.

Mike, now that you have your Manhattan, it is time to take everything we discussed and apply it to the real world. How do you invest without losing money? I am going to give you my secret. But first ask yourself why is it a secret? Why is the financial industry not talking about this? Why are the people who called themselves financial advisors not talking to you about this?

I'm not particularly bright. Why was I able to figure this out? I can only conclude that the financial industry must know this secret. This is the only conclusion possible. The only possible answer is that they have voluntarily decided not to provide this information.

This became obvious to me when I attended a presentation from Manulife. They had hired a Math PHD to show the impact of volatility when it was interacting with the timing of retirement income. The PHD showed that volatility could erase more than 50% of your retirement assets when making withdrawals just because of timing. If this was true, I came to the conclusion that the reverse had to be also true. Volatility when interacting with the timing of your deposits could also erase 50% of your future retirement assets. Scary isn't it? And nobody is talking about this.

I ran the numbers which was not so difficult. The math was simple and you do not have to be an actuary to build the mathematic model. God, I was surprised by the results. I found out what the financial industry is trying very hard to hide.

Managing the timing of your deposits through what I called Planned Investing increases retirement assets by 125% to 150% compared to regular investment strategy such as Dollar Cost Averaging (which is in reality not an investment strategy).

Again as I contemplate the mathematical model behind Planned Investing, I have to wonder: Why is this not known? The math is not terribly complex. Anyone could figure this out…Why is this not mentioned to investors? I don't know of one investor who would not be interested in increasing their assets at retirement without taking more risks? Why are investment advisors not discussing this with clients? Considering the fees charged for investment advice, you would think that advisors would jump at the opportunity to demonstrate their value…

Maybe it is because advisors are not advisors after all. They are just salesmen. As salesmen, their objectives are to charge the most commission for the least amount of service and time allocated to clients. As a result, most investment advice is based on belief and dogma. The investment of money is based on beliefs which trump scientific facts while marketed reasoning dictates what we believe to be true.

What is Planned Investing? How do you use this strategy to avoid losing hundreds of thousands of dollars in retirement assets? Here are the steps required:

1. **Get a retirement plan.** It is important to understand the nature of a plan. Do you sail Mike? You do! Good! A retirement plan is the course that you will navigate to reach point B from point A.

2. **Understand that the retirement plan is static.** Like sailing, even if you plot a course, chances are you will deviate from this course because of wind, tides, presence of other boats. Sailing a boat is a dynamic experience. The same thing applies to investing.

3. **Be ready to act.** The plan allows you to know how far from

course you are at any given moment and therefore allows you to take the appropriate action to get back on course.

4. **How do you get back on course?** You first have to recognize that when planning your retirement, you are dealing and will be managing **THREE pools of money**. Each pool of money is different and must be managed differently. The first pool of money is the money that is not invested including the deposits that you will be making in your investment. The second pool of money is the money that is invested. The third pool of money is created when you are 10 years from retirement. This pool of money will provide you with the short term retirement income you need. It should be worth at least 5 years of income.

5. **Manage your transitions.** When money is deposited into an investment it is called a transition. When money is withdrawn from an investment to provide a retirement income it is also called a transition. Most money is lost at transitions. Therefore it is imperative that you actively manage your transitions. You can get away with being passive with the money already invested and which will remain invested. However you can't do this for deposits and withdrawals.

6. **Establish investment policies.** You manage money through the setup of investment policies. The first priority is always to first manage the transitions. There will be a separate investment policy for your deposits. There will be a separate investment policy for the money that is already invested and a final separate investment policy for the money that will be withdrawn if you are approaching retirement. These policies will differ from each other but again, managing the transitions comes before managing the money that is already invested.

7. **Be prepared and act accordingly.** Your investment policies will dictate what course of action or what is the correction needed if you deviate from the course you have plotted through your retirement plan.

Now let's look at an example. Assume we have a 40 year old

named John with $10,000 in a RRSP. He will be making deposits of $500 every month. It is year 2000 and he will be investing into a fund linked to the TSX.

First step is to do a retirement plan. His plan is done at 5% and it shows that his RRSP will be worth $169,450 in 16 years. Now if John does not set an investment policy for his deposits and does not manage transition, in 2016, his RRSP based on historical returns will be way off course and will only have a value of $139,845. He is in trouble. It is not at age 55, 10 years away from retirement, that you start addressing a retirement shortfall. Ten years away from retirement, you do not have the flexibility to correct your course to reach destination. This would entail taking a lot of risks which he should not be taking.

What if John had been told about Planned Investing? He would have set up his investment policies. Let's assume he sets up an investment policy for his deposits while deciding to use a buy and hold approach for the money that is invested. His investment policy is based on the multiple of 5. It means that for any year where he is 105% of plan, he will reduce his contribution to the TSX fund by 20% and will instead deposit this money into a money market fund (assuming a 2% rate of return). For example, if he is 115% of plan, he would reduce his deposits in the TSX fund by 60% for that year and putting $300 in the Money Market fund and $200 in the TSX fund.

His investment policy also states that when he is below plan, the same "multiple of 5" strategy will be used. The policy dictates that he will increase his deposits into the TSX fund by withdrawing from the Money Market fund when he is below plan. If he is 95% of plan, he will take $100 out of Money Market, adding it to the deposit of $500 going into the TSX fund.

Using the TSX returns from 2000 to 2016 and by applying this simple investment policy, his RRSP would be worth $173,941 by the end of 2016. He would be ahead of plan. I have a summary table to show you…

Table 1. Retirement Plan 5% versus Dollar Cost Averaging versus Planned Investing

Year	Total Invested	Retirement Plan 5%	Dollar Cost Averaging invested value TSX	Planned Investing invested value TSX	Planned Investing Money Market value	Planned Investing Total value
1	$16,000	$16,677	$12,693	$12,693	$0	$12,693
5	$40,000	$46,978	$47,305	$47,305	$0	$47,305
10	$70,000	$94,435	$82,925	$82,595	$13,375	$95,970
16	$106,000	$169,451	$139,846	$164,077	$9,864	$173,941

Many in the financial industry would call this market timing. This is ridiculous. In this approach we don't care about what the market does. We only care about where we are in relation to our plan. Any corrections is established ahead of time and automatically applied when results deviate from plan. It removes any emotion out of the decision. There is no timing.

Why would the financial industry consider this to be market timing? The answer is simple. Planned Investing generates changes and increases the number of transactions. This strategy requires time since the advisor must monitor the investment in relation to its individual plan. For an advisor, the best financial plan is the financial plan that sits on the shelf to be dusted off once in a while. Transactions decrease profits and commissions. Since we are dealing with salesmen, they don't want to manage your money; they want to profit from it.

There is only one person who cares about your money and it is you. Only you can do this. You can't afford to pay high fees to people who don't want to actively look after your money. Passive investing creates bad results. Active investing without a plan creates bad results. Only planning, being prepared and knowing what to do will create the right results. You can't afford to pay fees to advisors and fund managers, losing 25 to 40% of your retirement assets, to an industry which does not want to take the time to look after your money.

Mike, I was very conservative in my example. If I had used an investment policy for the money invested instead of relying on buying and holding, I would have increased my results by another 25%. This is scarier for the industry. Having money actively moving out of a fund because of an advisor who is actively managing the money of his clients is prohibited. I had the chance to meet an advisor in Quebec who was employing this strategy. He was delivering returns to his clients of 11% and above while the average in the industry was around 2%. He would literally have to send thousands of faxes to change the investment allocations of his clients. At Head Office, they hated him. He created work and was increasing costs. Today, he is not in the industry anymore. They found a way to get rid of him.

My final tip is simple. While you need to know the questions, you don't necessarily need to know the answers. While knowing the questions will not ensure your financial success, it will ensure that you are not the victim of a financial disaster. Avoiding a financial disaster is the first and most important step towards achieving any kind of financial security.

ABOUT THE AUTHOR

Richard Proteau has worked in the financial industry all of his professional life. After earning different financial industry designations such as FLMI, CLU, RHU, and CFP, Richard wrote many articles regarding fiscal laws pertaining to investments and life insurance. His last position was as Vice President of sales in the province of Quebec for a large insurance company. He has been a speaker at many industry conferences.

He is currently involved in the financial industry as an advocate for the consumer rights of investors and insurance policy holders. He is currently lobbying for changes to regulations of segregated funds to protect consumers against the illegal commercial practices used by advisors and insurers.

Richard is also working on submitting a report on the commercial practices of insurance companies. The first important conclusion of this report is that insurance companies have monopolized the influence over the decisional process regarding the changes needed to modernize regulations in this industry. The consumer is not represented. In fact, the power of the insurance lobby is so great that it has prevented any meaningful changes in this industry for the last 40 years with the objective of limiting the sophistication of the consumer's response in relation to toxic financial products these companies have sold.

Richard Proteau first book was "UNRAVELING THE UNIVERSAL LIFE SCAM" which proved the criminal activities of insurance companies used in selling Universal Life.

Blog: https://911insurance.wordpress.com/
Facebook: https://www.facebook.com/consumerights.ca/
Website: www.consumerights.ca
YouTube: https://www.youtube.com/watch?v=O4IjpaP06nY
Amazon: https://www.amazon.com/Unraveling-Universal-Life-Shorter-Truth/dp/1503246167
Kobo: https://store.kobobooks.com/en-CA/ebook/unraveling-the-universal-life-scam

www.ingramcontent.com/pod-product-compliance
Lightning Source LLC
Chambersburg PA
CBHW070242190526
45169CB00001B/271